LIFE ALCHEMY

2.0

THE DAILY WORKBOOK FOR CONTINUED LIFE TRANSFORMATION

Dr. Dale Ellwein

"Success is the sum of small efforts, repeated day in and day out."

Robert Collier

NAME   _____

PHONE   _____

ADDRESS   _____

                _____

START DATE   _____

COMPLETION   _____

PREFACE

Congratulation!

By now you have experienced a jump into your future, greater than you probably ever expected. You have taken some bold steps, eaten a few frogs, and shifted your life in gear to create the life of gold that you deserve.

You are born to succeed! You are a success!
This book contains your next chapter in life (at least the next 3 months of your life).

Thank you for finding the value of this daily practice.
Thank you for picking up where you left off, and rocking forward with *Life Alchemy 2.0*.

Because you are already an awesome success, and you have completed Life Alchemy 1.0, we are going to jump right in. No fluff, no explanations, and no excuses! Let's go!

M T W T F S S

Date: _____

If you are just coming off of Life Alchemy 1.0, you can just copy in the "Weekly Re-Focus" from week 13

If you have let some time laps since you completed Life Alchemy 1.0, roll up your sleeves and start dreaming up your ideal life out of the ethers of your mind. Let's make some magic!

Answer This Question

If there were no rules, and I could not fail, what would my life be like? Describe this future life in detail and in writing.

_____

_____

_____

_____

_____

_____

_____

_____

Look through your future life. Feels pretty good, doesn't it? Now, fill in the blank...

If I only accomplish _____,
my future life would surely come to be.

Whatever single thing you write on the above line you can use as your Primary Objective throughout this book. My intention for you is that you either move closer to achieving your Primary Objective, or you get it, in the next 3 months. The next question to answer is: What do you suppose it would feel like if you achieved your Primary Objective? Describe how it would feel as if you have accomplished it now.

_____

_____

My Primary Objective

_____

_____

ACTION STEPS FOR TODAY

High Priority

1. _____

2. _____

3. _____

Medium Priority

1. _____

2. _____

3. _____

Low Priority

_____

_____

_____

_____

_____

_____

This is the big formula in the alchemy of life: know what you want, visualize it as if it has come to be, and feel it as if it has been accomplished. Of course, now you must take action towards its completion. Write your Primary Objective in the box above and set your Action Steps for Today. Be sure to include at least one thing in your High Priority list that you can do today that will get you a step closer to your future ideal life.

Weekly Goal Focus:

Today I am grateful for...

_____
_____
_____
_____
_____
_____
_____
_____
_____

How was my day? Did I feel good about my performance? What did I learn? Did I have a new insight? What would I do differently?

_____
_____
_____
_____
_____
_____
_____
_____

NOTES AND REFLECTIONS FROM TODAY

What was my energy level today? (lowest to highest) 1 2 3 4 5 6 7 8 9 10

If not a "10", what will I do tomorrow to make it closer to a "10"? _____

Tomorrow we will jump into eating your frog and your habits. For now, let's look at "For Tomorrow."

"There are so many ways to fail but only one way to succeed; NEVER GIVE UP!"

Johni Pangalila

FOR TOMORROW

_____
_____
_____
_____

DAILY PREVIEW
DAY 2

M T W T F S S

Date: _____

MY PRIMARY OBJECTIVE

[_____]

The most important thing I can do today to take me a step closer to my Primary Objective is _____.

The most important thing I can do today to take me a step closer to my Primary Objective is _____.

The most important thing I can do today to take me a step closer to my Primary Objective is _____.

The most important thing I can do today to take me a step closer to my Primary Objective is _____.

My new habit I'm developing (eliminating) is... _____

MORNING THOUGHTS AND INSPIRATIONS

My biggest frog to eat today...

_____

ACTION STEPS FOR TODAY

High Priority
1. _____
2. _____
3. _____

Medium Priority
1. _____
2. _____
3. _____

Low Priority
_____
_____
_____
_____
_____
_____

In which area(s) do I want to improve the most today?

Mental Health

Spiritual Health

Career Health

Physical Health

Social Health

Family Health

Financial Health

Weekly Goal Focus:

Today I am grateful for...

_____

_____

_____

_____

_____

_____

_____

_____

_____

How was my day? Did I feel good about my performance? What did I learn? Did I have a new insight? What would I do differently?

_____

_____

_____

_____

_____

_____

_____

_____

NOTES AND REFLECTIONS FROM TODAY

What was my energy level today? (lowest to highest) 1 2 3 4 5 6 7 8 9 10

If not a "10", what will I do tomorrow to make it closer to a "10"? _____

I ate my frog today: Yes   No

What Time? _____

I did my new habit: Yes   No

What Time? _____

FOR TOMORROW

_____

_____

_____

_____

"For true success ask yourself these four questions: Why? Why not? Why not me? Why not now?"

James Allen

DAILY PREVIEW
DAY 3

M T W T F S S

Date: _____

MY PRIMARY OBJECTIVE

[   ]

The most important thing I can do today to take me a step closer to my Primary Objective is _____ .

The most important thing I can do today to take me a step closer to my Primary Objective is _____ .

The most important thing I can do today to take me a step closer to my Primary Objective is _____ .

The most important thing I can do today to take me a step closer to my Primary Objective is _____ .

My new habit I'm developing (eliminating) is... _____

MORNING THOUGHTS AND INSPIRATIONS

My biggest frog to eat today...

_____

ACTION STEPS FOR TODAY

High Priority

1. _____
2. _____
3. _____

Medium Priority

1. _____
2. _____
3. _____

Low Priority

_____
_____
_____
_____
_____
_____

In which area(s) do I want to improve the most today?

Mental Health

Spiritual Health

Career Health

Physical Health

Social Health

Family Health

Financial Health

Weekly Goal Focus:

Today I am grateful for...

_____

_____

_____

_____

_____

_____

_____

_____

_____

How was my day? Did I feel good about my performance? What did I learn? Did I have a new insight? What would I do differently?

_____

_____

_____

_____

_____

_____

_____

_____

NOTES AND REFLECTIONS FROM TODAY

What was my energy level today? (lowest to highest) 1 2 3 4 5 6 7 8 9 10

If not a "10", what will I do tomorrow to make it closer to a "10"? _____

I ate my frog today: Yes   No

What Time? _____

I did my new habit: Yes   No

What Time? _____

FOR TOMORROW

_____

_____

_____

_____

"Nobody ever wrote down a plan to be broke, fat, lazy, or stupid. Those things are what happen when you don't have a plan."

Larry Winget

DAILY PREVIEW
DAY 4

M T W T F S S

Date: _____

MY PRIMARY OBJECTIVE

The most important thing I can do today to take me a step closer to my Primary Objective is _____.

The most important thing I can do today to take me a step closer to my Primary Objective is _____.

The most important thing I can do today to take me a step closer to my Primary Objective is _____.

The most important thing I can do today to take me a step closer to my Primary Objective is _____.

My new habit I'm developing (eliminating) is... _____

MORNING THOUGHTS AND INSPIRATIONS

My biggest frog to eat today...
_____

ACTION STEPS FOR TODAY

High Priority
1. _____
2. _____
3. _____

Medium Priority
1. _____
2. _____
3. _____

Low Priority
_____
_____
_____
_____
_____
_____

In which area(s) do I want to improve the most today?

Mental Health

Spiritual Health

Career Health

Physical Health

Social Health

Family Health

Financial Health

Today I am grateful for...

_____
_____
_____
_____
_____
_____
_____
_____

How was my day? Did I feel good about my performance? What did I learn? Did I have a new insight? What would I do differently?

_____
_____
_____
_____
_____
_____
_____
_____
_____

NOTES AND REFLECTIONS FROM TODAY

What was my energy level today? (lowest to highest) 1 2 3 4 5 6 7 8 9 10

If not a "10", what will I do tomorrow to make it closer to a "10"? _____

I ate my frog today: Yes No

I did my new habit: Yes No

What Time? _____

What Time? _____

FOR TOMORROW

_____
_____
_____
_____

"Though no one can go back and make a brand new start, anyone can start from now and make a brand new ending."

Anonymous

DAILY PREVIEW
DAY 5

M T W T F S S

Date: _____

MY PRIMARY OBJECTIVE

The most important thing I can do today to take me a step closer to my Primary Objective is _____.

The most important thing I can do today to take me a step closer to my Primary Objective is _____.

The most important thing I can do today to take me a step closer to my Primary Objective is _____.

The most important thing I can do today to take me a step closer to my Primary Objective is _____.

My new habit I'm developing (eliminating) is... _____

MORNING THOUGHTS AND INSPIRATIONS

My biggest frog to eat today...

_____

ACTION STEPS FOR TODAY

High Priority
1. _____
2. _____
3. _____

Medium Priority
1. _____
2. _____
3. _____

Low Priority
_____
_____
_____
_____
_____
_____

In which area(s) do I want to improve the most today?

Mental Health

Spiritual Health

Career Health

Physical Health

Social Health

Family Health

Financial Health

Weekly Goal Focus:

Today I am grateful for...

_____
_____
_____
_____
_____
_____
_____
_____

How was my day? Did I feel good about my performance? What did I learn? Did I have a new insight? What would I do differently?

_____
_____
_____
_____
_____
_____
_____
_____

NOTES AND REFLECTIONS FROM TODAY

What was my energy level today? (lowest to highest) 1 2 3 4 5 6 7 8 9 10

If not a "10", what will I do tomorrow to make it closer to a "10"? _____

I ate my frog today: Yes   No

What Time? _____

I did my new habit: Yes   No

What Time? _____

FOR TOMORROW

_____
_____
_____
_____

"Success means having the courage, the determination, and the will to become the person you believe you were meant to be."

George Sheehan

DAILY PREVIEW
DAY 6

My biggest frog to eat today...
_____

ACTION STEPS FOR TODAY

MY PRIMARY OBJECTIVE

The most important thing I can do today to take me a step closer to my Primary Objective is _____.

The most important thing I can do today to take me a step closer to my Primary Objective is _____.

The most important thing I can do today to take me a step closer to my Primary Objective is _____.

The most important thing I can do today to take me a step closer to my Primary Objective is _____.

My new habit I'm developing (eliminating) is... _____

MORNING THOUGHTS AND INSPIRATIONS

High Priority
1. _____
2. _____
3. _____

Medium Priority
1. _____
2. _____
3. _____

Low Priority
_____
_____
_____
_____
_____
_____

In which area(s) do I want to improve the most today?

Mental Health

Spiritual Health

Career Health

Physical Health

Social Health

Family Health

Financial Health

Weekly Goal Focus:

Today I am grateful for...

_____
_____
_____
_____
_____
_____
_____
_____
_____

How was my day? Did I feel good about my performance? What did I learn? Did I have a new insight? What would I do differently?

_____
_____
_____
_____
_____
_____
_____
_____

NOTES AND REFLECTIONS FROM TODAY

What was my energy level today? (lowest to highest) 1 2 3 4 5 6 7 8 9 10

If not a "10", what will I do tomorrow to make it closer to a "10"? _____

I ate my frog today: Yes   No

What Time? _____

I did my new habit: Yes   No

What Time? _____

FOR TOMORROW

_____
_____
_____
_____

"Success is not the key to happiness. Happiness is the key to success. If you love what you are doing, you will be successful."

Herman Cain

M T W T F S S

Date: _____

MY PRIMARY OBJECTIVE 👉

[   ]

The most important thing I can do today to take me a step closer to my Primary Objective is _____.

The most important thing I can do today to take me a step closer to my Primary Objective is _____.

The most important thing I can do today to take me a step closer to my Primary Objective is _____.

The most important thing I can do today to take me a step closer to my Primary Objective is _____.

My new habit I'm developing (eliminating) is... _____

MORNING THOUGHTS AND INSPIRATIONS ☀

[   ]

My biggest frog to eat today...

_____

ACTION STEPS FOR TODAY 🚩

High Priority

1. _____
2. _____
3. _____

Medium Priority

1. _____
2. _____
3. _____

Low Priority

_____
_____
_____
_____
_____
_____

In which area(s) do I want to improve the most today?

Mental Health

Spiritual Health

Career Health

Physical Health

Social Health

Family Health

Financial Health

Weekly Goal Focus:

Today I am grateful for...

_____
_____
_____
_____
_____
_____
_____
_____
_____

How was my day? Did I feel good about my performance? What did I learn? Did I have a new insight? What would I do differently?

_____
_____
_____
_____
_____
_____
_____
_____

NOTES AND REFLECTIONS FROM TODAY

What was my energy level today? (lowest to highest)   1 2 3 4 5 6 7 8 9 10

If not a "10", what will I do tomorrow to make it closer to a "10"? _____

I ate my frog today: Yes   No

What Time? _____

I did my new habit: Yes   No

What Time? _____

"I find my greatest pleasure, and so my reward, in the work that precedes what the world calls success."

Thomas Edison

FOR TOMORROW

_____
_____
_____
_____

WEEKLY CHECK-IN
WEEK 1

The Purpose of the Weekly Check-In is to...

1) Check-in with your progress throughout the week.

2) Re-focus for the upcoming week.

3) Get inspired for the future.

THE CHECK-IN

What have I accomplished since last week? What were the two most important things that I learned this week? Is there anything that I would have done differently? If so, what?

_____
_____
_____
_____
_____

What are my wins or victories since last week?

_____
_____
_____

What's the highlight (or low-light) of my week?

_____
_____
_____

What am I thankful for this week?

_____
_____
_____

The place I feel stuck is

_____
_____
_____

In which area(s) did I grow the most last week?

Mental Health

Spiritual Health

Career Health

Physical Health

Social Health

Family Health

Financial Health

What was my average energy level for the week?

1 2 3 4 5 6 7 8 9 10

What number do I want it to be next week?

1 2 3 4 5 6 7 8 9 10

How often did you eat your frog?

1 2 3 4 5 6

On a 1 - 10 scale, 1 being low and 10 being high, how grateful have I been feeling this last week?

1 2 3 4 5 6 7 8 9 10

How did I do with my new habit building/eliminating?

_____
_____
_____

Every week, we will be re-focusing on our future life. So, take a moment and fill this in again. There will be a few questions after you finish.

If there were no rules, and I could not fail, what would my life be like?

Describe your future life in detail and in writing...

_____

_____

_____

_____

_____

_____

_____

When you wrote this out again, how did you feel? Were you excited? Were you bored? Did your vision evolve? Was it different than before? Was there more detail or less? Did you even do this exercise? If not, how come?

_____

_____

_____

Set Your Primary Objective for next week.

Look through your future life. Now, fill in the blank...

If I only accomplish _____ next week, my future life would surely come to be.

This is your Primary Objective for the next week.

(As a special note, if by chance you miss a few days or stray from the process of working in this book on a daily basis, when you are ready to get started again, go to the next Weekly Check-In section and start there. This is an excellent place to jump back in and get going again.)

Take a moment and fill in the days of the week for the next week.

Go on to Day 8 and be amazing!

DAILY PREVIEW
DAY 8

M T W T F S S

Date: _____

MY PRIMARY OBJECTIVE

The most important thing I can do today to take me a step closer to my Primary Objective is _____ .

The most important thing I can do today to take me a step closer to my Primary Objective is _____ .

The most important thing I can do today to take me a step closer to my Primary Objective is _____ .

The most important thing I can do today to take me a step closer to my Primary Objective is _____ .

My new habit I'm developing (eliminating) is... _____

MORNING THOUGHTS AND INSPIRATIONS

My biggest frog to eat today...
_____

ACTION STEPS FOR TODAY

High Priority
1. _____
2. _____
3. _____

Medium Priority
1. _____
2. _____
3. _____

Low Priority
_____
_____
_____
_____
_____
_____

In which area(s) do I want to improve the most today?

Mental Health

Spiritual Health

Career Health

Physical Health

Social Health

Family Health

Financial Health

Weekly Goal Focus:

Today I am grateful for...

_____

_____

_____

_____

_____

_____

_____

_____

_____

How was my day? Did I feel good about my performance? What did I learn? Did I have a new insight? What would I do differently?

_____

_____

_____

_____

_____

_____

_____

_____

NOTES AND REFLECTIONS FROM TODAY

What was my energy level today? (lowest to highest) 1 2 3 4 5 6 7 8 9 10

If not a "10", what will I do tomorrow to make it closer to a "10"? _____

I ate my frog today: Yes   No

What Time? _____

I did my new habit: Yes   No

What Time? _____

FOR TOMORROW

_____

_____

_____

_____

"An Unfailing Success Plan: At each day's end write down the six most important things to do tomorrow; number them in order of importance, and then do them."

Anonymous

DAILY PREVIEW
DAY 9

M T W T F S S

Date: _____

MY PRIMARY OBJECTIVE

[_____]

The most important thing I can do today to take me a step closer to my Primary Objective is _____.

The most important thing I can do today to take me a step closer to my Primary Objective is _____.

The most important thing I can do today to take me a step closer to my Primary Objective is _____.

The most important thing I can do today to take me a step closer to my Primary Objective is _____.

My new habit I'm developing (eliminating) is... _____

MORNING THOUGHTS AND INSPIRATIONS

My biggest frog to eat today...

_____

ACTION STEPS FOR TODAY

High Priority
1. _____
2. _____
3. _____

Medium Priority
1. _____
2. _____
3. _____

Low Priority
_____
_____
_____
_____
_____
_____

In which area(s) do I want to improve the most today?

Mental Health

Spiritual Health

Career Health

Physical Health

Social Health

Family Health

Financial Health

Weekly Goal Focus:

_____

Today I am grateful for...

_____

_____

_____

_____

_____

_____

_____

_____

_____

How was my day? Did I feel good about my performance? What did I learn? Did I have a new insight? What would I do differently?

_____

_____

_____

_____

_____

_____

_____

_____

NOTES AND REFLECTIONS FROM TODAY

What was my energy level today? (lowest to highest) 1 2 3 4 5 6 7 8 9 10

If not a "10", what will I do tomorrow to make it closer to a "10"? _____

I ate my frog today: Yes   No

What Time? _____

I did my new habit: Yes   No

What Time? _____

"What you get by achieving your goals is not as important as what you become by achieving your goals."

Goethe

FOR TOMORROW

_____

_____

_____

_____

M T W T F S S

Date: _____

MY PRIMARY OBJECTIVE

[ ]

The most important thing I can do today to take me a step closer to my Primary Objective is _____.

The most important thing I can do today to take me a step closer to my Primary Objective is _____.

The most important thing I can do today to take me a step closer to my Primary Objective is _____.

The most important thing I can do today to take me a step closer to my Primary Objective is _____.

My new habit I'm developing (eliminating) is... _____

MORNING THOUGHTS AND INSPIRATIONS

My biggest frog to eat today...
_____

ACTION STEPS FOR TODAY

High Priority

1. _____
2. _____
3. _____

Medium Priority

1. _____
2. _____
3. _____

Low Priority

_____
_____
_____
_____
_____
_____

In which area(s) do I want to improve the most today?

Mental Health

Spiritual Health

Career Health

Physical Health

Social Health

Family Health

Financial Health

Today I am grateful for...

_____

_____

_____

_____

_____

_____

_____

_____

_____

How was my day? Did I feel good about my performance? What did I learn? Did I have a new insight? What would I do differently?

_____

_____

_____

_____

_____

_____

_____

_____

NOTES AND REFLECTIONS FROM TODAY

What was my energy level today? (lowest to highest) 1 2 3 4 5 6 7 8 9 10

If not a "10", what will I do tomorrow to make it closer to a "10"? _____

I ate my frog today: Yes   No

What Time? _____

I did my new habit: Yes   No

What Time? _____

"Accept responsibility for your life. Know that it is you who will get you where you want to go, no one else."

Les Brown

FOR TOMORROW

_____

_____

_____

_____

DAILY PREVIEW
DAY 11

M T W T F S S

Date: _____

MY PRIMARY OBJECTIVE

[   ]

The most important thing I can do today to take me a step closer to my Primary Objective is _____.

The most important thing I can do today to take me a step closer to my Primary Objective is _____.

The most important thing I can do today to take me a step closer to my Primary Objective is _____.

The most important thing I can do today to take me a step closer to my Primary Objective is _____.

My new habit I'm developing (eliminating) is... _____

MORNING THOUGHTS AND INSPIRATIONS

My biggest frog to eat today...

_____

ACTION STEPS FOR TODAY

High Priority
1. _____
2. _____
3. _____

Medium Priority
1. _____
2. _____
3. _____

Low Priority
_____
_____
_____
_____
_____
_____

In which area(s) do I want to improve the most today?

Mental Health

Spiritual Health

Career Health

Physical Health

Social Health

Family Health

Financial Health

Weekly Goal Focus:

Today I am grateful for...

_____

_____

_____

_____

_____

_____

_____

_____

_____

How was my day? Did I feel good about my performance? What did I learn? Did I have a new insight? What would I do differently?

_____

_____

_____

_____

_____

_____

_____

_____

NOTES AND REFLECTIONS FROM TODAY

What was my energy level today? (lowest to highest)   1 2 3 4 5 6 7 8 9 10

If not a "10", what will I do tomorrow to make it closer to a "10"? _____

I ate my frog today: Yes   No

What Time? _____

I did my new habit: Yes   No

What Time? _____

"Learn how to be happy with what you have while you pursue all that you want."

Jim Rohn

FOR TOMORROW

_____

_____

_____

_____

DAILY PREVIEW
DAY 12

M T W T F S S

Date: _____

MY PRIMARY OBJECTIVE 👉 [   ]

The most important thing I can do today to take me a step closer to my Primary Objective is _____.

The most important thing I can do today to take me a step closer to my Primary Objective is _____.

The most important thing I can do today to take me a step closer to my Primary Objective is _____.

The most important thing I can do today to take me a step closer to my Primary Objective is _____.

My new habit I'm developing (eliminating) is... _____

MORNING THOUGHTS AND INSPIRATIONS ☀

My biggest frog to eat today...
_____

ACTION STEPS FOR TODAY 🚩

High Priority
1. _____
2. _____
3. _____

Medium Priority
1. _____
2. _____
3. _____

Low Priority
_____
_____
_____
_____
_____
_____

In which area(s) do I want to improve the most today?

Mental Health

Spiritual Health

Career Health

Physical Health

Social Health

Family Health

Financial Health

Weekly Goal Focus:

Today I am grateful for...

_____

_____

_____

_____

_____

_____

_____

_____

_____

How was my day? Did I feel good about my performance? What did I learn? Did I have a new insight? What would I do differently?

_____

_____

_____

_____

_____

_____

_____

_____

NOTES AND REFLECTIONS FROM TODAY

What was my energy level today? (lowest to highest)   1 2 3 4 5 6 7 8 9 10

If not a "10", what will I do tomorrow to make it closer to a "10"? _____

I ate my frog today: Yes   No

What Time? _____

I did my new habit: Yes   No

What Time? _____

"Every achiever I have ever met says, 'My life turned around when I began to believe in me."

Robert Schuller

FOR TOMORROW

_____

_____

_____

_____

DAILY PREVIEW
DAY 13

M T W T F S S

Date: _____

MY PRIMARY OBJECTIVE 👆

The most important thing I can do today to take me a step closer to my Primary Objective is _____.

The most important thing I can do today to take me a step closer to my Primary Objective is _____.

The most important thing I can do today to take me a step closer to my Primary Objective is _____.

The most important thing I can do today to take me a step closer to my Primary Objective is _____.

My new habit I'm developing (eliminating) is... _____

MORNING THOUGHTS AND INSPIRATIONS ☀

My biggest frog to eat today...

_____

ACTION STEPS FOR TODAY ⚑

High Priority

1. _____
2. _____
3. _____

Medium Priority

1. _____
2. _____
3. _____

Low Priority

_____
_____
_____
_____
_____
_____

In which area(s) do I want to improve the most today?

Mental Health

Spiritual Health

Career Health

Physical Health

Social Health

Family Health

Financial Health

Weekly Goal Focus:

Today I am grateful for...

_____
_____
_____
_____
_____
_____
_____
_____
_____
_____

How was my day? Did I feel good about my performance? What did I learn? Did I have a new insight? What would I do differently?

_____
_____
_____
_____
_____
_____
_____
_____
_____

✏ NOTES AND REFLECTIONS FROM TODAY

What was my energy level today? (lowest to highest)   1 2 3 4 5 6 7 8 9 10

If not a "10", what will I do tomorrow to make it closer to a "10"? _____

I ate my frog today: Yes   No

What Time? _____

I did my new habit: Yes   No

What Time? _____

FOR TOMORROW

_____
_____
_____
_____

"You miss 100% of the shots you don't take."

Wayne Gretzky

DAILY PREVIEW
DAY 14

M T W T F S S

Date: _____

MY PRIMARY OBJECTIVE

[ ]

The most important thing I can do today to take me a step closer to my Primary Objective is _____.

The most important thing I can do today to take me a step closer to my Primary Objective is _____.

The most important thing I can do today to take me a step closer to my Primary Objective is _____.

The most important thing I can do today to take me a step closer to my Primary Objective is _____.

My new habit I'm developing (eliminating) is... _____

MORNING THOUGHTS AND INSPIRATIONS

My biggest frog to eat today...

_____

ACTION STEPS FOR TODAY

High Priority

1. _____
2. _____
3. _____

Medium Priority

1. _____
2. _____
3. _____

Low Priority

_____
_____
_____
_____
_____
_____

In which area(s) do I want to improve the most today?

Mental Health

Spiritual Health

Career Health

Physical Health

Social Health

Family Health

Financial Health

Weekly Goal Focus:

Today I am grateful for...

_____
_____
_____
_____
_____
_____
_____
_____
_____

How was my day? Did I feel good about my performance? What did I learn? Did I have a new insight? What would I do differently?

_____
_____
_____
_____
_____
_____
_____
_____

NOTES AND REFLECTIONS FROM TODAY

What was my energy level today? (lowest to highest) 1 2 3 4 5 6 7 8 9 10

If not a "10", what will I do tomorrow to make it closer to a "10"? _____

I ate my frog today: Yes   No

What Time? _____

I did my new habit: Yes   No

What Time? _____

"Keep steadily before you the fact that all true success depends at last upon yourself."

Theodore T. Hunger

FOR TOMORROW

_____
_____
_____
_____

WEEKLY CHECK-INS
WEEK 2

The Purpose of the Weekly Check-In is to...

1) *Check-in with your progress throughout the week.*

2) *Re-focus for the upcoming week.*

3) *Get inspired for the future.*

THE CHECK-IN

What have I accomplished since last week? What were the two most important things that I learned this week? Is there anything that I would have done differently? If so, what?

_____
_____
_____
_____
_____

What are my wins or victories since last week?

_____
_____
_____

What's the highlight (or low-light) of my week?

_____
_____
_____

What am I thankful for this week?

_____
_____
_____

The place I feel stuck is

_____
_____
_____

In which area(s) did I grow the most last week?

Mental Health

Spiritual Health

Career Health

Physical Health

Social Health

Family Health

Financial Health

What was my average energy level for the week?

1 2 3 4 5 6 7 8 9 10

What number do I want it to be next week?

1 2 3 4 5 6 7 8 9 10

How often did you eat your frog?

1 2 3 4 5 6 7

On a 1 - 10 scale, 1 being low and 10 being high, how grateful have I been feeling this last week?

1 2 3 4 5 6 7 8 9 10

How did I do with my new habit building/eliminating?

_____
_____
_____

Every week, we will be re-focusing on our future life. So, take a moment and fill this in again. There will be a few questions after you finish.

If there were no rules, and I could not fail, what would my life be like?

Describe your future life in detail and in writing...

_____

_____

_____

_____

_____

_____

_____

When you wrote this out again, how did you feel? Were you excited? Were you bored? Did your vision evolve? Was it different than before? Was there more detail or less? Did you even do this exercise? If not, how come?

_____

_____

_____

Look through your future life. Now, fill in the blank...

If I only accomplish _____ next week, my future life would surely come to be.

This is your Primary Objective for the next week.

Take a moment and fill in the days of the week for the next week.

Go on to Day 15 and be amazing!

DAILY PREVIEW
DAY 15

M T W T F S S

Date: _____

My biggest frog to eat today...

_____

MY PRIMARY OBJECTIVE

[   ]

The most important thing I can do today to take me a step closer to my Primary Objective is _____.

The most important thing I can do today to take me a step closer to my Primary Objective is _____.

The most important thing I can do today to take me a step closer to my Primary Objective is _____.

The most important thing I can do today to take me a step closer to my Primary Objective is _____.

My new habit I'm developing (eliminating) is... _____

MORNING THOUGHTS AND INSPIRATIONS

ACTION STEPS FOR TODAY

High Priority

1. _____
2. _____
3. _____

Medium Priority

1. _____
2. _____
3. _____

Low Priority

_____
_____
_____
_____
_____
_____

In which area(s) do I want to improve the most today?

Mental Health

Spiritual Health

Career Health

Physical Health

Social Health

Family Health

Financial Health

Weekly Goal Focus:

Today I am grateful for...

_____
_____
_____
_____
_____
_____
_____
_____
_____

How was my day? Did I feel good about my performance? What did I learn? Did I have a new insight? What would I do differently?

_____
_____
_____
_____
_____
_____
_____
_____

NOTES AND REFLECTIONS FROM TODAY

What was my energy level today? (lowest to highest) 1 2 3 4 5 6 7 8 9 10

If not a "10", what will I do tomorrow to make it closer to a "10"? _____

I ate my frog today: Yes   No

What Time? _____

I did my new habit: Yes   No

What Time? _____

FOR TOMORROW

_____
_____
_____
_____

"If you set your goals ridiculously high and it's a failure, you will fail above everyone else's success."

James Cameron

DAILY PREVIEW
DAY 16

M T W T F S S

Date: _____

MY PRIMARY OBJECTIVE

[ ]

The most important thing I can do today to take me a step closer to my Primary Objective is _____.

The most important thing I can do today to take me a step closer to my Primary Objective is _____.

The most important thing I can do today to take me a step closer to my Primary Objective is _____.

The most important thing I can do today to take me a step closer to my Primary Objective is _____.

My new habit I'm developing (eliminating) is... _____

MORNING THOUGHTS AND INSPIRATIONS

My biggest frog to eat today...

_____

ACTION STEPS FOR TODAY

High Priority
1. _____
2. _____
3. _____

Medium Priority
1. _____
2. _____
3. _____

Low Priority
_____
_____
_____
_____
_____
_____

In which area(s) do I want to improve the most today?

Mental Health

Spiritual Health

Career Health

Physical Health

Social Health

Family Health

Financial Health

Weekly Goal Focus:

Today I am grateful for...

_____

_____

_____

_____

_____

_____

_____

_____

_____

How was my day? Did I feel good about my performance? What did I learn? Did I have a new insight? What would I do differently?

_____

_____

_____

_____

_____

_____

_____

_____

NOTES AND REFLECTIONS FROM TODAY

What was my energy level today? (lowest to highest)   1 2 3 4 5 6 7 8 9 10

If not a "10", what will I do tomorrow to make it closer to a "10"? _____

I ate my frog today: Yes   No

What Time? _____

I did my new habit: Yes   No

What Time? _____

FOR TOMORROW

_____

_____

_____

_____

"We are what we repeatedly do. Excellence, therefore, is not an act but a habit."

Aristotle

M T W T F S S

Date: _____

My biggest frog to eat today...

_____

ACTION STEPS FOR TODAY

MY PRIMARY OBJECTIVE

The most important thing I can do today to take me a step closer to my Primary Objective is _____.

The most important thing I can do today to take me a step closer to my Primary Objective is _____.

The most important thing I can do today to take me a step closer to my Primary Objective is _____.

The most important thing I can do today to take me a step closer to my Primary Objective is _____.

My new habit I'm developing (eliminating) is... _____

MORNING THOUGHTS AND INSPIRATIONS

High Priority

1. _____
2. _____
3. _____

Medium Priority

1. _____
2. _____
3. _____

Low Priority

_____
_____
_____
_____
_____
_____

In which area(s) do I want to improve the most today?

Mental Health

Spiritual Health

Career Health

Physical Health

Social Health

Family Health

Financial Health

Today I am grateful for...

_____

_____

_____

_____

_____

_____

_____

_____

_____

How was my day? Did I feel good about my performance? What did I learn? Did I have a new insight? What would I do differently?

_____

_____

_____

_____

_____

_____

_____

_____

_____

NOTES AND REFLECTIONS FROM TODAY

What was my energy level today? (lowest to highest) 1 2 3 4 5 6 7 8 9 10

If not a "10", what will I do tomorrow to make it closer to a "10"? _____

I ate my frog today: Yes   No

What Time? _____

I did my new habit: Yes   No

What Time? _____

"The only person you are destined to become is the person you decide to be."
Ralph Waldo Emerson

FOR TOMORROW

_____

_____

_____

_____

M T W T F S S

Date: _____

MY PRIMARY OBJECTIVE

The most important thing I can do today to take me a step closer to my Primary Objective is _____.

The most important thing I can do today to take me a step closer to my Primary Objective is _____.

The most important thing I can do today to take me a step closer to my Primary Objective is _____.

The most important thing I can do today to take me a step closer to my Primary Objective is _____.

My new habit I'm developing (eliminating) is... _____

MORNING THOUGHTS AND INSPIRATIONS

My biggest frog to eat today...

_____

ACTION STEPS FOR TODAY

High Priority

1. _____
2. _____
3. _____

Medium Priority

1. _____
2. _____
3. _____

Low Priority

_____
_____
_____
_____
_____
_____

In which area(s) do I want to improve the most today?

Mental Health

Spiritual Health

Career Health

Physical Health

Social Health

Family Health

Financial Health

DAILY REVIEW
DAY 18

Today I am grateful for...

_____
_____
_____
_____
_____
_____
_____
_____
_____
_____

How was my day? Did I feel good about my performance? What did I learn? Did I have a new insight? What would I do differently?

_____
_____
_____
_____
_____
_____
_____
_____
_____

NOTES AND REFLECTIONS FROM TODAY

What was my energy level today? (lowest to highest) 1 2 3 4 5 6 7 8 9 10

If not a "10", what will I do tomorrow to make it closer to a "10"? _____

I ate my frog today: Yes   No

What Time? _____

I did my new habit: Yes   No

What Time? _____

FOR TOMORROW

_____
_____
_____
_____

"The thing always happens that you really believe in; and the belief in a thing makes it happen."

Frank Loyd Wright

DAILY PREVIEW
DAY 19

M T W T F S S

Date: _____

MY PRIMARY OBJECTIVE

☞

[ ]

The most important thing I can do today to take me a step closer to my Primary Objective is _____.

The most important thing I can do today to take me a step closer to my Primary Objective is _____.

The most important thing I can do today to take me a step closer to my Primary Objective is _____.

The most important thing I can do today to take me a step closer to my Primary Objective is _____.

My new habit I'm developing (eliminating) is... _____

MORNING THOUGHTS AND INSPIRATIONS

☀

My biggest frog to eat today...
_____

ACTION STEPS FOR TODAY ⚑

High Priority
1. _____
2. _____
3. _____

Medium Priority
1. _____
2. _____
3. _____

Low Priority
_____
_____
_____
_____
_____
_____

In which area(s) do I want to improve the most today?

Mental Health

Spiritual Health

Career Health

Physical Health

Social Health

Family Health

Financial Health

Weekly Goal Focus:

Today I am grateful for...

_____
_____
_____
_____
_____
_____
_____
_____

How was my day? Did I feel good about my performance? What did I learn? Did I have a new insight? What would I do differently?

_____
_____
_____
_____
_____
_____
_____
_____

NOTES AND REFLECTIONS FROM TODAY

What was my energy level today? (lowest to highest) 1 2 3 4 5 6 7 8 9 10

If not a "10", what will I do tomorrow to make it closer to a "10"? _____

I ate my frog today: Yes   No

I did my new habit: Yes   No

What Time? _____

What Time? _____

FOR TOMORROW

_____
_____
_____
_____

"Youth is curious, and success is a game for curiosity seekers. Stay young!"

BJ Palmer

DAILY PREVIEW
DAY 20

M T W T F S S

Date: _____

MY PRIMARY OBJECTIVE

The most important thing I can do today to take me a step closer to my Primary Objective is _____.

The most important thing I can do today to take me a step closer to my Primary Objective is _____.

The most important thing I can do today to take me a step closer to my Primary Objective is _____.

The most important thing I can do today to take me a step closer to my Primary Objective is _____.

My new habit I'm developing (eliminating) is... _____

MORNING THOUGHTS AND INSPIRATIONS

My biggest frog to eat today...
_____

ACTION STEPS FOR TODAY

High Priority

1. _____
2. _____
3. _____

Medium Priority

1. _____
2. _____
3. _____

Low Priority

_____

_____

_____

_____

_____

_____

In which area(s) do I want to improve the most today?

Mental Health

Spiritual Health

Career Health

Physical Health

Social Health

Family Health

Financial Health

Weekly Goal Focus:

Today I am grateful for...

_____

_____

_____

_____

_____

_____

_____

_____

How was my day? Did I feel good about my performance? What did I learn? Did I have a new insight? What would I do differently?

_____

_____

_____

_____

_____

_____

_____

_____

NOTES AND REFLECTIONS FROM TODAY

What was my energy level today? (lowest to highest) 1 2 3 4 5 6 7 8 9 10

If not a "10", what will I do tomorrow to make it closer to a "10"? _____

I ate my frog today: Yes   No

What Time? _____

I did my new habit: Yes   No

What Time? _____

"When I let go of what I am, I become what I might be."

Lao Tzu

FOR TOMORROW

_____

_____

_____

_____

DAILY PREVIEW
DAY 21

M T W T F S S

Date: _____

MY PRIMARY OBJECTIVE

[ ]

The most important thing I can do today to take me a step closer to my Primary Objective is _____.

The most important thing I can do today to take me a step closer to my Primary Objective is _____.

The most important thing I can do today to take me a step closer to my Primary Objective is _____.

The most important thing I can do today to take me a step closer to my Primary Objective is _____.

My new habit I'm developing (eliminating) is... _____

MORNING THOUGHTS AND INSPIRATIONS

My biggest frog to eat today...

_____

ACTION STEPS FOR TODAY

High Priority

1. _____
2. _____
3. _____

Medium Priority

1. _____
2. _____
3. _____

Low Priority

_____
_____
_____
_____
_____
_____

In which area(s) do I want to improve the most today?

Mental Health

Spiritual Health

Career Health

Physical Health

Social Health

Family Health

Financial Health

48

Today I am grateful for...

_____
_____
_____
_____
_____
_____
_____
_____
_____

How was my day? Did I feel good about my performance? What did I learn? Did I have a new insight? What would I do differently?

_____
_____
_____
_____
_____
_____
_____
_____

NOTES AND REFLECTIONS FROM TODAY

What was my energy level today? (lowest to highest)   1 2 3 4 5 6 7 8 9 10

If not a "10", what will I do tomorrow to make it closer to a "10"? _____

I ate my frog today: Yes   No

What Time? _____

I did my new habit: Yes   No

What Time? _____

FOR TOMORROW

_____
_____
_____
_____

"The surest way not to fail is to determine to succeed."
Richard Brinsley Sheridan

WEEKLY CHECK-INS
WEEK 3

The Purpose of the Weekly Check-In is to...

1) Check-in with your progress throughout the week.

2) Re-focus for the upcoming week.

3) Get inspired for the future.

THE CHECK-IN

What have I accomplished since last week? What were the two most important things that I learned this week? Is there anything that I would have done differently? If so, what?

_____
_____
_____
_____
_____

What are my wins or victories since last week?

_____
_____
_____

What's the highlight (or low-light) of my week?

_____
_____
_____

What am I thankful for this week?

_____
_____
_____

The place I feel stuck is

_____
_____
_____

In which area(s) did I grow the most last week?

Mental Health

Spiritual Health

Career Health

Physical Health

Social Health

Family Health

Financial Health

What was my average energy level for the week?

1 2 3 4 5 6 7 8 9 10

What number do I want it to be next week?

1 2 3 4 5 6 7 8 9 10

How often did you eat your frog?

1 2 3 4 5 6 7

On a 1 - 10 scale, 1 being low and 10 being high, how grateful have I been feeling this last week?

1 2 3 4 5 6 7 8 9 10

How did I do with my new habit building/eliminating?

_____
_____
_____

Every week, we will be re-focusing on our future life. So, take a moment and fill this in again. There will be a few questions after you finish.

If there were no rules, and I could not fail, what would my life be like?

Describe your future life in detail and in writing...

_____

_____

_____

_____

_____

_____

When you wrote this out again, how did you feel? Were you excited? Were you bored? Did your vision evolve? Was it different than before? Was there more detail or less? Did you even do this exercise? If not, how come?

_____

_____

_____

Look through your future life. Now, fill in the blank...

If I only accomplish _____ next week, my future life would surely come to be.

This is your Primary Objective for the next week.

Take a moment and fill in the days of the week for the next week.

Go on to Day 22 and be amazing!

DAILY PREVIEW
DAY 22

M T W T F S S

Date: _____

MY PRIMARY OBJECTIVE

[   ]

The most important thing I can do today to take me a step closer to my Primary Objective is _____.

The most important thing I can do today to take me a step closer to my Primary Objective is _____.

The most important thing I can do today to take me a step closer to my Primary Objective is _____.

The most important thing I can do today to take me a step closer to my Primary Objective is _____.

My new habit I'm developing (eliminating) is... _____

MORNING THOUGHTS AND INSPIRATIONS

My biggest frog to eat today...
_____

ACTION STEPS FOR TODAY

High Priority
1. _____
2. _____
3. _____

Medium Priority
1. _____
2. _____
3. _____

Low Priority
_____
_____
_____
_____
_____
_____

In which area(s) do I want to improve the most today?

Mental Health

Spiritual Health

Career Health

Physical Health

Social Health

Family Health

Financial Health

Weekly Goal Focus:

Today I am grateful for...

_____
_____
_____
_____
_____
_____
_____
_____
_____

How was my day? Did I feel good about my performance? What did I learn? Did I have a new insight? What would I do differently?

_____
_____
_____
_____
_____
_____
_____
_____

NOTES AND REFLECTIONS FROM TODAY

What was my energy level today? (lowest to highest) 1 2 3 4 5 6 7 8 9 10

If not a "10", what will I do tomorrow to make it closer to a "10"? _____

I ate my frog today: Yes   No

What Time? _____

I did my new habit: Yes   No

What Time? _____

"Some people dream of success… while others wake up and work hard at it."
Author Unknown

FOR TOMORROW

_____
_____
_____
_____

DAILY PREVIEW
DAY 23

M T W T F S S

Date: _____

MY PRIMARY OBJECTIVE

[_____]

The most important thing I can do today to take me a step closer to my Primary Objective is _____.

The most important thing I can do today to take me a step closer to my Primary Objective is _____.

The most important thing I can do today to take me a step closer to my Primary Objective is _____.

The most important thing I can do today to take me a step closer to my Primary Objective is _____.

My new habit I'm developing (eliminating) is... _____

MORNING THOUGHTS AND INSPIRATIONS

My biggest frog to eat today...
_____

ACTION STEPS FOR TODAY

High Priority
1. _____
2. _____
3. _____

Medium Priority
1. _____
2. _____
3. _____

Low Priority
_____
_____
_____
_____
_____
_____

In which area(s) do I want to improve the most today?

Mental Health

Spiritual Health

Career Health

Physical Health

Social Health

Family Health

Financial Health

Weekly Goal Focus:

Today I am grateful for...

_____
_____
_____
_____
_____
_____
_____
_____
_____

How was my day? Did I feel good about my performance? What did I learn? Did I have a new insight? What would I do differently?

_____
_____
_____
_____
_____
_____
_____
_____
_____

NOTES AND REFLECTIONS FROM TODAY

What was my energy level today? (lowest to highest) 1 2 3 4 5 6 7 8 9 10

If not a "10", what will I do tomorrow to make it closer to a "10"? _____

I ate my frog today: Yes   No

What Time? _____

I did my new habit: Yes   No

What Time? _____

"The mind is everything. What you think you become."

Buddha

FOR TOMORROW

_____
_____
_____
_____

DAILY PREVIEW
DAY 24

M T W T F S S

Date: _____

MY PRIMARY OBJECTIVE

[_____]

The most important thing I can do today to take me a step closer to my Primary Objective is _____.

The most important thing I can do today to take me a step closer to my Primary Objective is _____.

The most important thing I can do today to take me a step closer to my Primary Objective is _____.

The most important thing I can do today to take me a step closer to my Primary Objective is _____.

My new habit I'm developing (eliminating) is... _____

MORNING THOUGHTS AND INSPIRATIONS

My biggest frog to eat today...

_____

ACTION STEPS FOR TODAY

High Priority
1. _____
2. _____
3. _____

Medium Priority
1. _____
2. _____
3. _____

Low Priority
_____
_____
_____
_____
_____
_____

In which area(s) do I want to improve the most today?

Mental Health

Spiritual Health

Career Health

Physical Health

Social Health

Family Health

Financial Health

Today I am grateful for...

_____
_____
_____
_____
_____
_____
_____
_____
_____

How was my day? Did I feel good about my performance? What did I learn? Did I have a new insight? What would I do differently?

_____
_____
_____
_____
_____
_____
_____
_____

NOTES AND REFLECTIONS FROM TODAY

What was my energy level today? (lowest to highest) 1 2 3 4 5 6 7 8 9 10

If not a "10", what will I do tomorrow to make it closer to a "10"? _____

I ate my frog today: Yes   No

What Time? _____

I did my new habit: Yes   No

What Time? _____

"Here is a test to find out whether your mission in life is complete. If you're still alive, it isn't."

Lauren Bacall

FOR TOMORROW

_____
_____
_____
_____

DAILY PREVIEW
DAY 25

M T W T F S S

Date: _____

MY PRIMARY OBJECTIVE

The most important thing I can do today to take me a step closer to my Primary Objective is _____.

The most important thing I can do today to take me a step closer to my Primary Objective is _____.

The most important thing I can do today to take me a step closer to my Primary Objective is _____.

The most important thing I can do today to take me a step closer to my Primary Objective is _____.

My new habit I'm developing (eliminating) is... _____

MORNING THOUGHTS AND INSPIRATIONS

My biggest frog to eat today...

_____

ACTION STEPS FOR TODAY

High Priority
1. _____
2. _____
3. _____

Medium Priority
1. _____
2. _____
3. _____

Low Priority
_____
_____
_____
_____
_____
_____

In which area(s) do I want to improve the most today?

Mental Health

Spiritual Health

Career Health

Physical Health

Social Health

Family Health

Financial Health

Weekly Goal Focus:

Today I am grateful for...

_____

_____

_____

_____

_____

_____

_____

_____

How was my day? Did I feel good about my performance? What did I learn? Did I have a new insight? What would I do differently?

_____

_____

_____

_____

_____

_____

_____

NOTES AND REFLECTIONS FROM TODAY

What was my energy level today? (lowest to highest)   1 2 3 4 5 6 7 8 9 10

If not a "10", what will I do tomorrow to make it closer to a "10"? _____

I ate my frog today: Yes   No

What Time? _____

I did my new habit: Yes   No

What Time? _____

"The only failure one (wo)man should fear, is the failure to do his (her) best."
D.D. Palmer

FOR TOMORROW

_____

_____

_____

_____

M T W T F S S

Date: _____

MY PRIMARY OBJECTIVE

The most important thing I can do today to take me a step closer to my Primary Objective is _____.

The most important thing I can do today to take me a step closer to my Primary Objective is _____.

The most important thing I can do today to take me a step closer to my Primary Objective is _____.

The most important thing I can do today to take me a step closer to my Primary Objective is _____.

My new habit I'm developing (eliminating) is... _____

MORNING THOUGHTS AND INSPIRATIONS

My biggest frog to eat today...

_____

ACTION STEPS FOR TODAY

High Priority
1. _____
2. _____
3. _____

Medium Priority
1. _____
2. _____
3. _____

Low Priority
_____
_____
_____
_____
_____
_____

In which area(s) do I want to improve the most today?

Mental Health

Spiritual Health

Career Health

Physical Health

Social Health

Family Health

Financial Health

DAILY REVIEW
DAY 26

Today I am grateful for...

_____
_____
_____
_____
_____
_____
_____
_____
_____

How was my day? Did I feel good about my performance? What did I learn? Did I have a new insight? What would I do differently?

_____
_____
_____
_____
_____
_____
_____
_____

NOTES AND REFLECTIONS FROM TODAY

What was my energy level today? (lowest to highest) 1 2 3 4 5 6 7 8 9 10

If not a "10", what will I do tomorrow to make it closer to a "10"? _____

I ate my frog today: Yes   No

What Time? _____

I did my new habit: Yes   No

What Time? _____

FOR TOMORROW

_____
_____
_____
_____

"Life isn't about getting and having, it's about giving and being."

Kevin Kruse

DAILY PREVIEW
DAY 27

M T W T F S S

Date: _____

MY PRIMARY OBJECTIVE

The most important thing I can do today to take me a step closer to my Primary Objective is _____.

The most important thing I can do today to take me a step closer to my Primary Objective is _____.

The most important thing I can do today to take me a step closer to my Primary Objective is _____.

The most important thing I can do today to take me a step closer to my Primary Objective is _____.

My new habit I'm developing (eliminating) is... _____

MORNING THOUGHTS AND INSPIRATIONS

My biggest frog to eat today...

_____

ACTION STEPS FOR TODAY

High Priority
1. _____
2. _____
3. _____

Medium Priority
1. _____
2. _____
3. _____

Low Priority
_____
_____
_____
_____
_____
_____

In which area(s) do I want to improve the most today?

Mental Health

Spiritual Health

Career Health

Physical Health

Social Health

Family Health

Financial Health

Weekly Goal Focus:

Today I am grateful for...

_____
_____
_____
_____
_____
_____
_____
_____
_____
_____

How was my day? Did I feel good about my performance? What did I learn? Did I have a new insight? What would I do differently?

_____
_____
_____
_____
_____
_____
_____
_____
_____

NOTES AND REFLECTIONS FROM TODAY

What was my energy level today? (lowest to highest) 1 2 3 4 5 6 7 8 9 10

If not a "10", what will I do tomorrow to make it closer to a "10"? _____

I ate my frog today: Yes   No

What Time? _____

I did my new habit: Yes   No

What Time? _____

FOR TOMORROW

_____
_____
_____
_____

"Opportunity is missed by most people because it is dressed in overalls and looks like work."

Thomas Edison

M T W T F S S

Date: _____

My biggest frog to eat today...

_____

ACTION STEPS FOR TODAY

MY PRIMARY OBJECTIVE

The most important thing I can do today to take me a step closer to my Primary Objective is _____.

The most important thing I can do today to take me a step closer to my Primary Objective is _____.

The most important thing I can do today to take me a step closer to my Primary Objective is _____.

The most important thing I can do today to take me a step closer to my Primary Objective is _____.

My new habit I'm developing (eliminating) is... _____

MORNING THOUGHTS AND INSPIRATIONS

High Priority
1. _____
2. _____
3. _____

Medium Priority
1. _____
2. _____
3. _____

Low Priority
_____
_____
_____
_____
_____
_____

In which area(s) do I want to improve the most today?

Mental Health

Spiritual Health

Career Health

Physical Health

Social Health

Family Health

Financial Health

Today I am grateful for...

_____
_____
_____
_____
_____
_____
_____
_____
_____
_____

How was my day? Did I feel good about my performance? What did I learn? Did I have a new insight? What would I do differently?

_____
_____
_____
_____
_____
_____
_____
_____

NOTES AND REFLECTIONS FROM TODAY

What was my energy level today? (lowest to highest) 1 2 3 4 5 6 7 8 9 10

If not a "10", what will I do tomorrow to make it closer to a "10"? _____

I ate my frog today: Yes   No

What Time? _____

I did my new habit: Yes   No

What Time? _____

"Your chances of success in any undertaking can always be measured by your belief in yourself."

Robert Collier

FOR TOMORROW

_____
_____
_____
_____

WEEKLY CHECK-INS
WEEK 4

The Purpose of the Weekly Check-In is to...

1) Check-in with your progress throughout the week.

2) Re-focus for the upcoming week.

3) Get inspired for the future.

THE CHECK-IN

What have I accomplished since last week? What were the two most important things that I learned this week? Is there anything that I would have done differently? If so, what?

_____
_____
_____
_____
_____

What are my wins or victories since last week?

_____
_____
_____

What's the highlight (or low-light) of my week?

_____
_____
_____

What am I thankful for this week?

_____
_____
_____

The place I feel stuck is

_____
_____
_____

In which area(s) did I grow the most last week?

Mental Health

Spiritual Health

Career Health

Physical Health

Social Health

Family Health

Financial Health

What was my average energy level for the week?

1 2 3 4 5 6 7 8 9 10

What number do I want it to be next week?

1 2 3 4 5 6 7 8 9 10

How often did you eat your frog?

1 2 3 4 5 6 7

On a 1 - 10 scale, 1 being low and 10 being high, how grateful have I been feeling this last week?

1 2 3 4 5 6 7 8 9 10

How did I do with my new habit building/eliminating?

_____
_____
_____

Every week, we will be re-focusing on our future life. So, take a moment and fill this in again. There will be a few questions after you finish.

If there were no rules, and I could not fail, what would my life be like?

Describe your future life in detail and in writing...

_____

_____

_____

_____

_____

_____

_____

When you wrote this out again, how did you feel? Were you excited? Were you bored? Did your vision evolve? Was it different than before? Was there more detail or less? Did you even do this exercise? If not, how come?

_____

_____

_____

Look through your future life. Now, fill in the blank...

If I only accomplish _____ next week, my future life would surely come to be.

This is your Primary Objective for the next week.

Take a moment and fill in the days of the week for the next week.

Go on to Day 29 and be amazing!

DAILY PREVIEW
DAY 29

M T W T F S S

Date: _____

MY PRIMARY OBJECTIVE

[blank box]

The most important thing I can do today to take me a step closer to my Primary Objective is _____.

The most important thing I can do today to take me a step closer to my Primary Objective is _____.

The most important thing I can do today to take me a step closer to my Primary Objective is _____.

The most important thing I can do today to take me a step closer to my Primary Objective is _____.

My new habit I'm developing (eliminating) is... _____

MORNING THOUGHTS AND INSPIRATIONS

My biggest frog to eat today...

_____

ACTION STEPS FOR TODAY

High Priority

1. _____
2. _____
3. _____

Medium Priority

1. _____
2. _____
3. _____

Low Priority

_____
_____
_____
_____
_____
_____

In which area(s) do I want to improve the most today?

Mental Health

Spiritual Health

Career Health

Physical Health

Social Health

Family Health

Financial Health

Today I am grateful for...

_____
_____
_____
_____
_____
_____
_____
_____
_____

How was my day? Did I feel good about my performance? What did I learn? Did I have a new insight? What would I do differently?

_____
_____
_____
_____
_____
_____
_____
_____

NOTES AND REFLECTIONS FROM TODAY

What was my energy level today? (lowest to highest) 1 2 3 4 5 6 7 8 9 10

If not a "10", what will I do tomorrow to make it closer to a "10"? _____

I ate my frog today: Yes   No

I did my new habit: Yes   No

What Time? _____

What Time? _____

"Give the world the best you have, and the best will come to you."

Madeline Bridge

FOR TOMORROW

_____
_____
_____
_____

DAILY PREVIEW
DAY 30

M T W T F S S

Date: _____

MY PRIMARY OBJECTIVE

☞ [_____]

The most important thing I can do today to take me a step closer to my Primary Objective is _____.

The most important thing I can do today to take me a step closer to my Primary Objective is _____.

The most important thing I can do today to take me a step closer to my Primary Objective is _____.

The most important thing I can do today to take me a step closer to my Primary Objective is _____.

My new habit I'm developing (eliminating) is... _____

MORNING THOUGHTS AND INSPIRATIONS

My biggest frog to eat today...

_____

ACTION STEPS FOR TODAY

High Priority

1. _____
2. _____
3. _____

Medium Priority

1. _____
2. _____
3. _____

Low Priority

_____
_____
_____
_____
_____
_____

In which area(s) do I want to improve the most today?

Mental Health

Spiritual Health

Career Health

Physical Health

Social Health

Family Health

Financial Health

Today I am grateful for...

_____
_____
_____
_____
_____
_____
_____
_____
_____

How was my day? Did I feel good about my performance? What did I learn? Did I have a new insight? What would I do differently?

_____
_____
_____
_____
_____
_____
_____
_____

NOTES AND REFLECTIONS FROM TODAY

What was my energy level today? (lowest to highest) 1 2 3 4 5 6 7 8 9 10

If not a "10", what will I do tomorrow to make it closer to a "10"? _____

I ate my frog today: Yes   No

What Time? _____

I did my new habit: Yes   No

What Time? _____

"It's never too late to be who you might have been."

George Elliot

FOR TOMORROW

_____
_____
_____
_____

DAILY PREVIEW
DAY 31

M T W T F S S

Date: _____

MY PRIMARY OBJECTIVE

[_____]

The most important thing I can do today to take me a step closer to my Primary Objective is _____.

The most important thing I can do today to take me a step closer to my Primary Objective is _____.

The most important thing I can do today to take me a step closer to my Primary Objective is _____.

The most important thing I can do today to take me a step closer to my Primary Objective is _____.

My new habit I'm developing (eliminating) is... _____

MORNING THOUGHTS AND INSPIRATIONS

My biggest frog to eat today...

_____

ACTION STEPS FOR TODAY

High Priority

1. _____
2. _____
3. _____

Medium Priority

1. _____
2. _____
3. _____

Low Priority

_____
_____
_____
_____
_____
_____

In which area(s) do I want to improve the most today?

Mental Health

Spiritual Health

Career Health

Physical Health

Social Health

Family Health

Financial Health

Today I am grateful for...

_____
_____
_____
_____
_____
_____
_____
_____
_____

How was my day? Did I feel good about my performance? What did I learn? Did I have a new insight? What would I do differently?

_____
_____
_____
_____
_____
_____
_____
_____

NOTES AND REFLECTIONS FROM TODAY

What was my energy level today? (lowest to highest) 1 2 3 4 5 6 7 8 9 10

If not a "10", what will I do tomorrow to make it closer to a "10"? _____

I ate my frog today: Yes   No

I did my new habit: Yes   No

What Time? _____

What Time? _____

"You may be disappointed if you fail, but you are doomed if you don't try."

Beverly Sills

FOR TOMORROW

_____
_____
_____
_____

DAILY PREVIEW
DAY 32

M T W T F S S

Date: _____

MY PRIMARY OBJECTIVE

The most important thing I can do today to take me a step closer to my Primary Objective is _____.

The most important thing I can do today to take me a step closer to my Primary Objective is _____.

The most important thing I can do today to take me a step closer to my Primary Objective is _____.

The most important thing I can do today to take me a step closer to my Primary Objective is _____.

My new habit I'm developing (eliminating) is... _____

MORNING THOUGHTS AND INSPIRATIONS

My biggest frog to eat today...

_____

ACTION STEPS FOR TODAY

High Priority

1. _____
2. _____
3. _____

Medium Priority

1. _____
2. _____
3. _____

Low Priority

_____
_____
_____
_____
_____
_____

In which area(s) do I want to improve the most today?

Mental Health

Spiritual Health

Career Health

Physical Health

Social Health

Family Health

Financial Health

Weekly Goal Focus:

Today I am grateful for...

_____
_____
_____
_____
_____
_____
_____
_____

How was my day? Did I feel good about my performance? What did I learn? Did I have a new insight? What would I do differently?

_____
_____
_____
_____
_____
_____
_____
_____

NOTES AND REFLECTIONS FROM TODAY

What was my energy level today? (lowest to highest) 1 2 3 4 5 6 7 8 9 10

If not a "10", what will I do tomorrow to make it closer to a "10"? _____

I ate my frog today: Yes No

What Time? _____

I did my new habit: Yes No

What Time? _____

FOR TOMORROW

_____
_____
_____
_____

"Talent is cheaper than table salt. What separates the talented individual from the successful one is a lot of hard work."

Stephen King

DAILY PREVIEW
DAY 33

M T W T F S S

Date: _____

MY PRIMARY OBJECTIVE

The most important thing I can do today to take me a step closer to my Primary Objective is _____.

The most important thing I can do today to take me a step closer to my Primary Objective is _____.

The most important thing I can do today to take me a step closer to my Primary Objective is _____.

The most important thing I can do today to take me a step closer to my Primary Objective is _____.

My new habit I'm developing (eliminating) is... _____

MORNING THOUGHTS AND INSPIRATIONS

My biggest frog to eat today...

_____

ACTION STEPS FOR TODAY

High Priority

1. _____
2. _____
3. _____

Medium Priority

1. _____
2. _____
3. _____

Low Priority

_____
_____
_____
_____
_____
_____

In which area(s) do I want to improve the most today?

Mental Health

Spiritual Health

Career Health

Physical Health

Social Health

Family Health

Financial Health

Weekly Goal Focus:

Today I am grateful for...

_____
_____
_____
_____
_____
_____
_____
_____
_____

How was my day? Did I feel good about my performance? What did I learn? Did I have a new insight? What would I do differently?

_____
_____
_____
_____
_____
_____
_____
_____

NOTES AND REFLECTIONS FROM TODAY

What was my energy level today? (lowest to highest) 1 2 3 4 5 6 7 8 9 10

If not a "10", what will I do tomorrow to make it closer to a "10"? _____

I ate my frog today: Yes   No

I did my new habit: Yes   No

What Time? _____

What Time? _____

"Everyone has a fair turn to be as great as (s)he pleases."

Jeremy Collier

FOR TOMORROW

_____
_____
_____
_____

DAILY PREVIEW
DAY 34

MY PRIMARY OBJECTIVE ☝

The most important thing I can do today to take me a step closer to my Primary Objective is _____.

The most important thing I can do today to take me a step closer to my Primary Objective is _____.

The most important thing I can do today to take me a step closer to my Primary Objective is _____.

The most important thing I can do today to take me a step closer to my Primary Objective is _____.

My new habit I'm developing (eliminating) is... _____

MORNING THOUGHTS AND INSPIRATIONS ☀

My biggest frog to eat today...
_____

ACTION STEPS FOR TODAY ⚑

High Priority
1. _____
2. _____
3. _____

Medium Priority
1. _____
2. _____
3. _____

Low Priority
_____
_____
_____
_____
_____
_____

In which area(s) do I want to improve the most today?

Mental Health

Spiritual Health

Career Health

Physical Health

Social Health

Family Health

Financial Health

Today I am grateful for...

_____

_____

_____

_____

_____

_____

_____

_____

_____

How was my day? Did I feel good about my performance? What did I learn? Did I have a new insight? What would I do differently?

_____

_____

_____

_____

_____

_____

_____

_____

NOTES AND REFLECTIONS FROM TODAY

What was my energy level today? (lowest to highest) 1 2 3 4 5 6 7 8 9 10

If not a "10", what will I do tomorrow to make it closer to a "10"? _____

I ate my frog today: Yes   No

What Time? _____

I did my new habit: Yes   No

What Time? _____

"You must do the very thing you think you cannot do."

Eleanor Roosevelt

FOR TOMORROW

_____

_____

_____

_____

DAILY PREVIEW
DAY 35

M T W T F S S

Date: _____

MY PRIMARY OBJECTIVE 👆

[_____]

The most important thing I can do today to take me a step closer to my Primary Objective is _____.

The most important thing I can do today to take me a step closer to my Primary Objective is _____.

The most important thing I can do today to take me a step closer to my Primary Objective is _____.

The most important thing I can do today to take me a step closer to my Primary Objective is _____.

My new habit I'm developing (eliminating) is... _____

MORNING THOUGHTS AND INSPIRATIONS ☀

My biggest frog to eat today...

_____

ACTION STEPS FOR TODAY 🚩

High Priority

1. _____
2. _____
3. _____

Medium Priority

1. _____
2. _____
3. _____

Low Priority

_____
_____
_____
_____
_____
_____

In which area(s) do I want to improve the most today?

Mental Health

Spiritual Health

Career Health

Physical Health

Social Health

Family Health

Financial Health

Weekly Goal Focus:

Today I am grateful for...

_____
_____
_____
_____
_____
_____
_____
_____
_____

How was my day? Did I feel good about my performance? What did I learn? Did I have a new insight? What would I do differently?

_____
_____
_____
_____
_____
_____
_____
_____

NOTES AND REFLECTIONS FROM TODAY

What was my energy level today? (lowest to highest) 1 2 3 4 5 6 7 8 9 10

If not a "10", what will I do tomorrow to make it closer to a "10"? _____

I ate my frog today: Yes   No

What Time? _____

I did my new habit: Yes   No

What Time? _____

"There is only one way to avoid criticism: do nothing, say nothing, and be nothing."

Aristotle

FOR TOMORROW

_____
_____
_____
_____

WEEKLY CHECK-INS
WEEK 5

The Purpose of the Weekly Check-In is to...

1) Check-in with your progress throughout the week.

2) Re-focus for the upcoming week.

3) Get inspired for the future.

THE CHECK-IN

What have I accomplished since last week? What were the two most important things that I learned this week? Is there anything that I would have done differently? If so, what?

_____
_____
_____
_____
_____

What are my wins or victories since last week?

_____
_____
_____

What's the highlight (or low-light) of my week?

_____
_____
_____

What am I thankful for this week?

_____
_____
_____

The place I feel stuck is

_____
_____
_____

In which area(s) did I grow the most last week?

Mental Health

Spiritual Health

Career Health

Physical Health

Social Health

Family Health

Financial Health

What was my average energy level for the week?

1 2 3 4 5 6 7 8 9 10

What number do I want it to be next week?

1 2 3 4 5 6 7 8 9 10

How often did you eat your frog?

1 2 3 4 5 6 7

On a 1 - 10 scale, 1 being low and 10 being high, how grateful have I been feeling this last week?

1 2 3 4 5 6 7 8 9 10

How did I do with my new habit building/eliminating?

_____
_____
_____

Every week, we will be re-focusing on our future life. So, take a moment and fill this in again. There will be a few questions after you finish.

RE-FOCUS
WEEK 5

If there were no rules, and I could not fail, what would my life be like?

Describe your future life in detail and in writing...

_____
_____
_____
_____
_____
_____
_____

When you wrote this out again, how did you feel? Were you excited? Were you bored? Did your vision evolve? Was it different than before? Was there more detail or less? Did you even do this exercise? If not, how come?

_____
_____
_____

Look through your future life. Now, fill in the blank...

If I only accomplish _____ next week, my future life would surely come to be.

This is your Primary Objective for the next week.

Take a moment and fill in the days of the week for the next week.

Go on to Day 36 and be amazing!

M T W T F S S

Date: _____

MY PRIMARY OBJECTIVE

The most important thing I can do today to take me a step closer to my Primary Objective is _____.

The most important thing I can do today to take me a step closer to my Primary Objective is _____.

The most important thing I can do today to take me a step closer to my Primary Objective is _____.

The most important thing I can do today to take me a step closer to my Primary Objective is _____.

My new habit I'm developing (eliminating) is... _____

MORNING THOUGHTS AND INSPIRATIONS

My biggest frog to eat today...

_____

ACTION STEPS FOR TODAY

High Priority
1. _____
2. _____
3. _____

Medium Priority
1. _____
2. _____
3. _____

Low Priority

_____

_____

_____

_____

_____

_____

In which area(s) do I want to improve the most today?

Mental Health

Spiritual Health

Career Health

Physical Health

Social Health

Family Health

Financial Health

Weekly Goal Focus:

Today I am grateful for...

_____

_____

_____

_____

_____

_____

_____

_____

How was my day? Did I feel good about my performance? What did I learn? Did I have a new insight? What would I do differently?

_____

_____

_____

_____

_____

_____

_____

_____

NOTES AND REFLECTIONS FROM TODAY

What was my energy level today? (lowest to highest) 1 2 3 4 5 6 7 8 9 10

If not a "10", what will I do tomorrow to make it closer to a "10"? _____

I ate my frog today: Yes   No

What Time? _____

I did my new habit: Yes   No

What Time? _____

"Success is a state of mind. If you want success, start thinking of yourself as a success."

Dr. Joyce Brothers

FOR TOMORROW

_____

_____

_____

_____

M T W T F S S

Date: _____

MY PRIMARY OBJECTIVE

The most important thing I can do today to take me a step closer to my Primary Objective is _____.

The most important thing I can do today to take me a step closer to my Primary Objective is _____.

The most important thing I can do today to take me a step closer to my Primary Objective is _____.

The most important thing I can do today to take me a step closer to my Primary Objective is _____.

My new habit I'm developing (eliminating) is... _____

MORNING THOUGHTS AND INSPIRATIONS

My biggest frog to eat today...

_____

ACTION STEPS FOR TODAY

High Priority
1. _____
2. _____
3. _____

Medium Priority
1. _____
2. _____
3. _____

Low Priority
_____
_____
_____
_____
_____
_____

In which area(s) do I want to improve the most today?

Mental Health

Spiritual Health

Career Health

Physical Health

Social Health

Family Health

Financial Health

DAILY REVIEW
DAY 37

Today I am grateful for...

_____
_____
_____
_____
_____
_____
_____
_____
_____

How was my day? Did I feel good about my performance? What did I learn? Did I have a new insight? What would I do differently?

_____
_____
_____
_____
_____
_____
_____

NOTES AND REFLECTIONS FROM TODAY

What was my energy level today? (lowest to highest) 1 2 3 4 5 6 7 8 9 10

If not a "10", what will I do tomorrow to make it closer to a "10"? _____

I ate my frog today: Yes   No

What Time? _____

I did my new habit: Yes   No

What Time? _____

"Every strike brings me closer to the next home run."

Babe Ruth

FOR TOMORROW

_____
_____
_____
_____

DAILY PREVIEW
DAY 38

M T W T F S S

Date: _____

MY PRIMARY OBJECTIVE

[_____]

The most important thing I can do today to take me a step closer to my Primary Objective is _____.

The most important thing I can do today to take me a step closer to my Primary Objective is _____.

The most important thing I can do today to take me a step closer to my Primary Objective is _____.

The most important thing I can do today to take me a step closer to my Primary Objective is _____.

My new habit I'm developing (eliminating) is... _____

MORNING THOUGHTS AND INSPIRATIONS

My biggest frog to eat today...

_____

ACTION STEPS FOR TODAY

High Priority
1. _____
2. _____
3. _____

Medium Priority
1. _____
2. _____
3. _____

Low Priority
_____
_____
_____
_____
_____
_____

In which area(s) do I want to improve the most today?

Mental Health

Spiritual Health

Career Health

Physical Health

Social Health

Family Health

Financial Health

DAILY REVIEW
DAY 38

Today I am grateful for...

_____
_____
_____
_____
_____
_____
_____
_____

How was my day? Did I feel good about my performance? What did I learn? Did I have a new insight? What would I do differently?

_____
_____
_____
_____
_____
_____
_____
_____

NOTES AND REFLECTIONS FROM TODAY

What was my energy level today? (lowest to highest) 1 2 3 4 5 6 7 8 9 10

If not a "10", what will I do tomorrow to make it closer to a "10"? _____

I ate my frog today: Yes   No

What Time? _____

I did my new habit: Yes   No

What Time? _____

FOR TOMORROW

_____
_____
_____
_____

"I am not a product of my circumstances. I am a product of my decisions."

Stephen Covey

DAILY PREVIEW
DAY 39

M T W T F S S

Date: _____

MY PRIMARY OBJECTIVE

The most important thing I can do today to take me a step closer to my Primary Objective is _____.

The most important thing I can do today to take me a step closer to my Primary Objective is _____.

The most important thing I can do today to take me a step closer to my Primary Objective is _____.

The most important thing I can do today to take me a step closer to my Primary Objective is _____.

My new habit I'm developing (eliminating) is... _____

MORNING THOUGHTS AND INSPIRATIONS

My biggest frog to eat today...

_____

ACTION STEPS FOR TODAY

High Priority

1. _____
2. _____
3. _____

Medium Priority

1. _____
2. _____
3. _____

Low Priority

_____
_____
_____
_____
_____
_____

In which area(s) do I want to improve the most today?

Mental Health

Spiritual Health

Career Health

Physical Health

Social Health

Family Health

Financial Health

Weekly Goal Focus:

Today I am grateful for...

_____

_____

_____

_____

_____

_____

_____

_____

How was my day? Did I feel good about my performance? What did I learn? Did I have a new insight? What would I do differently?

_____

_____

_____

_____

_____

_____

_____

_____

NOTES AND REFLECTIONS FROM TODAY

What was my energy level today? (lowest to highest) 1 2 3 4 5 6 7 8 9 10

If not a "10", what will I do tomorrow to make it closer to a "10"? _____

I ate my frog today: Yes   No

What Time? _____

I did my new habit: Yes   No

What Time? _____

"I have learned over the years that when one's mind is made up, this diminishes fear."

Rosa Parks

FOR TOMORROW

_____

_____

_____

_____

DAILY PREVIEW
DAY 40

MY PRIMARY OBJECTIVE

The most important thing I can do today to take me a step closer to my Primary Objective is _____.

The most important thing I can do today to take me a step closer to my Primary Objective is _____.

The most important thing I can do today to take me a step closer to my Primary Objective is _____.

The most important thing I can do today to take me a step closer to my Primary Objective is _____.

My new habit I'm developing (eliminating) is... _____

MORNING THOUGHTS AND INSPIRATIONS

My biggest frog to eat today...
_____

ACTION STEPS FOR TODAY

High Priority
1. _____
2. _____
3. _____

Medium Priority
1. _____
2. _____
3. _____

Low Priority
_____
_____
_____
_____
_____
_____

In which area(s) do I want to improve the most today?

Mental Health

Spiritual Health

Career Health

Physical Health

Social Health

Family Health

Financial Health

Weekly Goal Focus:

Today I am grateful for...

_____
_____
_____
_____
_____
_____
_____
_____
_____

How was my day? Did I feel good about my performance? What did I learn? Did I have a new insight? What would I do differently?

_____
_____
_____
_____
_____
_____
_____
_____

NOTES AND REFLECTIONS FROM TODAY

What was my energy level today? (lowest to highest) 1 2 3 4 5 6 7 8 9 10

If not a "10", what will I do tomorrow to make it closer to a "10"? _____

I ate my frog today: Yes   No

What Time? _____

I did my new habit: Yes   No

What Time? _____

"Nothing is impossible, the word itself says, "I'm possible!""

Audrey Hepburn

FOR TOMORROW

_____
_____
_____
_____

DAILY PREVIEW
DAY 41

M T W T F S S

Date: _____

MY PRIMARY OBJECTIVE

The most important thing I can do today to take me a step closer to my Primary Objective is _____.

The most important thing I can do today to take me a step closer to my Primary Objective is _____.

The most important thing I can do today to take me a step closer to my Primary Objective is _____.

The most important thing I can do today to take me a step closer to my Primary Objective is _____.

My new habit I'm developing (eliminating) is... _____

MORNING THOUGHTS AND INSPIRATIONS

My biggest frog to eat today...

_____

ACTION STEPS FOR TODAY

High Priority

1. _____
2. _____
3. _____

Medium Priority

1. _____
2. _____
3. _____

Low Priority

_____

_____

_____

_____

_____

_____

In which area(s) do I want to improve the most today?

Mental Health

Spiritual Health

Career Health

Physical Health

Social Health

Family Health

Financial Health

Today I am grateful for...

_____
_____
_____
_____
_____
_____
_____
_____
_____

How was my day? Did I feel good about my performance? What did I learn? Did I have a new insight? What would I do differently?

_____
_____
_____
_____
_____
_____
_____
_____

NOTES AND REFLECTIONS FROM TODAY

What was my energy level today? (lowest to highest) 1 2 3 4 5 6 7 8 9 10

If not a "10", what will I do tomorrow to make it closer to a "10"? _____

I ate my frog today: Yes   No

What Time? _____

I did my new habit: Yes   No

What Time? _____

"Either write something worth reading or do something worth writing."
Benjamin Franklin

FOR TOMORROW

_____
_____
_____
_____

DAILY PREVIEW
DAY 42

MY PRIMARY OBJECTIVE

[_____]

The most important thing I can do today to take me a step closer to my Primary Objective is _____.

The most important thing I can do today to take me a step closer to my Primary Objective is _____.

The most important thing I can do today to take me a step closer to my Primary Objective is _____.

The most important thing I can do today to take me a step closer to my Primary Objective is _____.

My new habit I'm developing (eliminating) is... _____

MORNING THOUGHTS AND INSPIRATIONS

My biggest frog to eat today...
_____

ACTION STEPS FOR TODAY

High Priority

1. _____
2. _____
3. _____

Medium Priority

1. _____
2. _____
3. _____

Low Priority

_____
_____
_____
_____
_____
_____

In which area(s) do I want to improve the most today?

Mental Health

Spiritual Health

Career Health

Physical Health

Social Health

Family Health

Financial Health

Weekly Goal Focus:

Today I am grateful for...

_____
_____
_____
_____
_____
_____
_____
_____
_____

How was my day? Did I feel good about my performance? What did I learn? Did I have a new insight? What would I do differently?

_____
_____
_____
_____
_____
_____
_____
_____

NOTES AND REFLECTIONS FROM TODAY

What was my energy level today? (lowest to highest) 1 2 3 4 5 6 7 8 9 10

If not a "10", what will I do tomorrow to make it closer to a "10"? _____

I ate my frog today: Yes   No

What Time? _____

I did my new habit: Yes   No

What Time? _____

"Dreaming, after all, is a form of planning."

Gloria Steinem

FOR TOMORROW

_____
_____
_____
_____

The Purpose of the Weekly Check-In is to...

1) Check-in with your progress throughout the week.

2) Re-focus for the upcoming week.

3) Get inspired for the future.

THE CHECK-IN

What have I accomplished since last week? What were the two most important things that I learned this week? Is there anything that I would have done differently? If so, what?

_____
_____
_____
_____
_____

What are my wins or victories since last week?

_____
_____
_____

What's the highlight (or low-light) of my week?

_____
_____
_____

What am I thankful for this week?

_____
_____
_____

The place I feel stuck is

_____
_____
_____

In which area(s) did I grow the most last week?

Mental Health

Spiritual Health

Career Health

Physical Health

Social Health

Family Health

Financial Health

What was my average energy level for the week?

1 2 3 4 5 6 7 8 9 10

What number do I want it to be next week?

1 2 3 4 5 6 7 8 9 10

How often did you eat your frog?

1 2 3 4 5 6 7

On a 1 - 10 scale, 1 being low and 10 being high, how grateful have I been feeling this last week?

1 2 3 4 5 6 7 8 9 10

How did I do with my new habit building/eliminating?

_____
_____
_____

Every week, we will be re-focusing on our future life. So, take a moment and fill this in again. There will be a few questions after you finish.

If there were no rules, and I could not fail, what would my life be like?

Describe your future life in detail and in writing...

_____

_____

_____

_____

_____

_____

_____

When you wrote this out again, how did you feel? Were you excited? Were you bored? Did your vision evolve? Was it different than before? Was there more detail or less? Did you even do this exercise? If not, how come?

_____

_____

_____

Look through your future life. Now, fill in the blank...

If I only accomplish _____ next week, my future life would surely come to be.

This is your Primary Objective for the next week.

Take a moment and fill in the days of the week for the next week.

Go on to Day 43 and be amazing!

DAILY PREVIEW
DAY 43

M T W T F S S

Date: _____

MY PRIMARY OBJECTIVE

[_____]

The most important thing I can do today to take me a step closer to my Primary Objective is _____.

The most important thing I can do today to take me a step closer to my Primary Objective is _____.

The most important thing I can do today to take me a step closer to my Primary Objective is _____.

The most important thing I can do today to take me a step closer to my Primary Objective is _____.

My new habit I'm developing (eliminating) is... _____

MORNING THOUGHTS AND INSPIRATIONS

My biggest frog to eat today...

_____

ACTION STEPS FOR TODAY

High Priority

1. _____
2. _____
3. _____

Medium Priority

1. _____
2. _____
3. _____

Low Priority

_____
_____
_____
_____
_____
_____

In which area(s) do I want to improve the most today?

Mental Health

Spiritual Health

Career Health

Physical Health

Social Health

Family Health

Financial Health

Weekly Goal Focus:

Today I am grateful for...

_____

_____

_____

_____

_____

_____

_____

_____

How was my day? Did I feel good about my performance? What did I learn? Did I have a new insight? What would I do differently?

_____

_____

_____

_____

_____

_____

_____

_____

NOTES AND REFLECTIONS FROM TODAY

What was my energy level today? (lowest to highest)   1 2 3 4 5 6 7 8 9 10

If not a "10", what will I do tomorrow to make it closer to a "10"? _____

I ate my frog today: Yes   No

What Time? _____

I did my new habit: Yes   No

What Time? _____

FOR TOMORROW

_____

_____

_____

_____

"Unless you try to do something beyond what you have already mastered, you will never grow."

Ralph Waldo Emerson

M T W T F S S

Date: _____

MY PRIMARY OBJECTIVE

The most important thing I can do today to take me a step closer to my Primary Objective is _____.

The most important thing I can do today to take me a step closer to my Primary Objective is _____.

The most important thing I can do today to take me a step closer to my Primary Objective is _____.

The most important thing I can do today to take me a step closer to my Primary Objective is _____.

My new habit I'm developing (eliminating) is... _____

MORNING THOUGHTS AND INSPIRATIONS

My biggest frog to eat today...
_____

ACTION STEPS FOR TODAY

High Priority
1. _____
2. _____
3. _____

Medium Priority
1. _____
2. _____
3. _____

Low Priority
_____
_____
_____
_____
_____
_____

In which area(s) do I want to improve the most today?

Mental Health

Spiritual Health

Career Health

Physical Health

Social Health

Family Health

Financial Health

Weekly Goal Focus:

Today I am grateful for...

_____

_____

_____

_____

_____

_____

_____

_____

_____

How was my day? Did I feel good about my performance? What did I learn? Did I have a new insight? What would I do differently?

_____

_____

_____

_____

_____

_____

_____

_____

NOTES AND REFLECTIONS FROM TODAY

What was my energy level today? (lowest to highest) 1 2 3 4 5 6 7 8 9 10

If not a "10", what will I do tomorrow to make it closer to a "10"? _____

I ate my frog today: Yes   No

What Time? _____

I did my new habit: Yes   No

What Time? _____

FOR TOMORROW

_____

_____

_____

_____

"Challenges are what make life interesting and overcoming them is what makes life meaningful."

Joshua J. Marine

DAILY PREVIEW
DAY 45

M T W T F S S

Date: _____

MY PRIMARY OBJECTIVE

The most important thing I can do today to take me a step closer to my Primary Objective is _____.

The most important thing I can do today to take me a step closer to my Primary Objective is _____.

The most important thing I can do today to take me a step closer to my Primary Objective is _____.

The most important thing I can do today to take me a step closer to my Primary Objective is _____.

My new habit I'm developing (eliminating) is... _____

MORNING THOUGHTS AND INSPIRATIONS

My biggest frog to eat today...

_____

ACTION STEPS FOR TODAY

High Priority
1. _____
2. _____
3. _____

Medium Priority
1. _____
2. _____
3. _____

Low Priority
_____
_____
_____
_____
_____
_____

In which area(s) do I want to improve the most today?

Mental Health

Spiritual Health

Career Health

Physical Health

Social Health

Family Health

Financial Health

Weekly Goal Focus:

Today I am grateful for...

_____

_____

_____

_____

_____

_____

_____

_____

How was my day? Did I feel good about my performance? What did I learn? Did I have a new insight? What would I do differently?

_____

_____

_____

_____

_____

_____

_____

_____

NOTES AND REFLECTIONS FROM TODAY

What was my energy level today? (lowest to highest) 1 2 3 4 5 6 7 8 9 10

If not a "10", what will I do tomorrow to make it closer to a "10"? _____

I ate my frog today: Yes   No

What Time? _____

I did my new habit: Yes   No

What Time? _____

FOR TOMORROW

_____

_____

_____

_____

"(Wo)Men are born to succeed, not fail."
Henry David Thoreau

M T W T F S S

Date: _____

MY PRIMARY OBJECTIVE

The most important thing I can do today to take me a step closer to my Primary Objective is _____.

The most important thing I can do today to take me a step closer to my Primary Objective is _____.

The most important thing I can do today to take me a step closer to my Primary Objective is _____.

The most important thing I can do today to take me a step closer to my Primary Objective is _____.

My new habit I'm developing (eliminating) is... _____

MORNING THOUGHTS AND INSPIRATIONS

My biggest frog to eat today...

_____

ACTION STEPS FOR TODAY

High Priority
1. _____
2. _____
3. _____

Medium Priority
1. _____
2. _____
3. _____

Low Priority
_____
_____
_____
_____
_____
_____

In which area(s) do I want to improve the most today?

Mental Health

Spiritual Health

Career Health

Physical Health

Social Health

Family Health

Financial Health

Weekly Goal Focus:

Today I am grateful for...

_____

_____

_____

_____

_____

_____

_____

_____

_____

How was my day? Did I feel good about my performance? What did I learn? Did I have a new insight? What would I do differently?

_____

_____

_____

_____

_____

_____

_____

_____

NOTES AND REFLECTIONS FROM TODAY

What was my energy level today? (lowest to highest) 1 2 3 4 5 6 7 8 9 10

If not a "10", what will I do tomorrow to make it closer to a "10"? _____

I ate my frog today: Yes   No

What Time? _____

I did my new habit: Yes   No

What Time? _____

FOR TOMORROW

_____

_____

_____

_____

"Strive not to be a success, but rather to be of value."

Albert Einstein

M T W T F S S

Date: _____

MY PRIMARY OBJECTIVE

[_____]

The most important thing I can do today to take me a step closer to my Primary Objective is _____.

The most important thing I can do today to take me a step closer to my Primary Objective is _____.

The most important thing I can do today to take me a step closer to my Primary Objective is _____.

The most important thing I can do today to take me a step closer to my Primary Objective is _____.

My new habit I'm developing (eliminating) is... _____

MORNING THOUGHTS AND INSPIRATIONS

My biggest frog to eat today...

_____

ACTION STEPS FOR TODAY

High Priority

1. _____
2. _____
3. _____

Medium Priority

1. _____
2. _____
3. _____

Low Priority

_____
_____
_____
_____
_____
_____

In which area(s) do I want to improve the most today?

Mental Health

Spiritual Health

Career Health

Physical Health

Social Health

Family Health

Financial Health

Weekly Goal Focus:

Today I am grateful for...

_____

_____

_____

_____

_____

_____

_____

_____

How was my day? Did I feel good about my performance? What did I learn? Did I have a new insight? What would I do differently?

_____

_____

_____

_____

_____

_____

_____

_____

NOTES AND REFLECTIONS FROM TODAY

What was my energy level today? (lowest to highest) 1 2 3 4 5 6 7 8 9 10

If not a "10", what will I do tomorrow to make it closer to a "10"? _____

I ate my frog today: Yes   No

What Time? _____

I did my new habit: Yes   No

What Time? _____

"Life isn't about finding yourself. Life is about creating yourself."

George Bernard Shaw

FOR TOMORROW

_____

_____

_____

_____

DAILY PREVIEW
DAY 48

M T W T F S S

Date: _____

MY PRIMARY OBJECTIVE

The most important thing I can do today to take me a step closer to my Primary Objective is _____.

The most important thing I can do today to take me a step closer to my Primary Objective is _____.

The most important thing I can do today to take me a step closer to my Primary Objective is _____.

The most important thing I can do today to take me a step closer to my Primary Objective is _____.

My new habit I'm developing (eliminating) is... _____

MORNING THOUGHTS AND INSPIRATIONS

My biggest frog to eat today...

_____

ACTION STEPS FOR TODAY

High Priority
1. _____
2. _____
3. _____

Medium Priority
1. _____
2. _____
3. _____

Low Priority
_____
_____
_____
_____
_____
_____

In which area(s) do I want to improve the most today?

Mental Health

Spiritual Health

Career Health

Physical Health

Social Health

Family Health

Financial Health

Weekly Goal Focus:

Today I am grateful for...

_____
_____
_____
_____
_____
_____
_____
_____

How was my day? Did I feel good about my performance? What did I learn? Did I have a new insight? What would I do differently?

_____
_____
_____
_____
_____
_____
_____

NOTES AND REFLECTIONS FROM TODAY

What was my energy level today? (lowest to highest) 1 2 3 4 5 6 7 8 9 10

If not a "10", what will I do tomorrow to make it closer to a "10"? _____

I ate my frog today: Yes   No

What Time? _____

I did my new habit: Yes   No

What Time? _____

"Your life does not get better by chance, it gets better by change."

Jim Rohn

FOR TOMORROW

_____
_____
_____
_____

DAILY PREVIEW
DAY 49

M T W T F S S

Date: _____

MY PRIMARY OBJECTIVE

The most important thing I can do today to take me a step closer to my Primary Objective is _____.

The most important thing I can do today to take me a step closer to my Primary Objective is _____.

The most important thing I can do today to take me a step closer to my Primary Objective is _____.

The most important thing I can do today to take me a step closer to my Primary Objective is _____.

My new habit I'm developing (eliminating) is... _____

MORNING THOUGHTS AND INSPIRATIONS

My biggest frog to eat today...

_____

ACTION STEPS FOR TODAY

High Priority
1. _____
2. _____
3. _____

Medium Priority
1. _____
2. _____
3. _____

Low Priority
_____
_____
_____
_____
_____
_____

In which area(s) do I want to improve the most today?

Mental Health

Spiritual Health

Career Health

Physical Health

Social Health

Family Health

Financial Health

Weekly Goal Focus:

Today I am grateful for...

_____
_____
_____
_____
_____
_____
_____
_____
_____

How was my day? Did I feel good about my performance? What did I learn? Did I have a new insight? What would I do differently?

_____
_____
_____
_____
_____
_____
_____
_____

NOTES AND REFLECTIONS FROM TODAY

What was my energy level today? (lowest to highest) 1 2 3 4 5 6 7 8 9 10

If not a "10", what will I do tomorrow to make it closer to a "10"? _____

I ate my frog today: Yes   No

What Time? _____

I did my new habit: Yes   No

What Time? _____

FOR TOMORROW

_____
_____
_____
_____

"Today you are You, that is truer than true. There is no one alive who is Youer than You."

Dr. Seuss

WEEKLY CHECK-INS
WEEK 7

The Purpose of the Weekly Check-In is to...

1) Check-in with your progress throughout the week.

2) Re-focus for the upcoming week.

3) Get inspired for the future.

THE CHECK-IN

What have I accomplished since last week? What were the two most important things that I learned this week? Is there anything that I would have done differently? If so, what?

_____
_____
_____
_____
_____

What are my wins or victories since last week?

_____
_____
_____

What's the highlight (or low-light) of my week?

_____
_____
_____

What am I thankful for this week?

_____
_____
_____

The place I feel stuck is

_____
_____
_____

In which area(s) did I grow the most last week?

Mental Health

Spiritual Health

Career Health

Physical Health

Social Health

Family Health

Financial Health

What was my average energy level for the week?

1 2 3 4 5 6 7 8 9 10

What number do I want it to be next week?

1 2 3 4 5 6 7 8 9 10

How often did you eat your frog?

1 2 3 4 5 6 7

On a 1 - 10 scale, 1 being low and 10 being high, how grateful have I been feeling this last week?

1 2 3 4 5 6 7 8 9 10

How did I do with my new habit building/eliminating?

_____
_____
_____

Every week, we will be re-focusing on our future life. So, take a moment and fill this in again. There will be a few questions after you finish.

If there were no rules, and I could not fail, what would my life be like?

Describe your future life in detail and in writing...

_____
_____
_____
_____
_____
_____
_____

When you wrote this out again, how did you feel? Were you excited? Were you bored? Did your vision evolve? Was it different than before? Was there more detail or less? Did you even do this exercise? If not, how come?

_____
_____
_____

Look through your future life. Now, fill in the blank...

If I only accomplish _____ next week, my future life would surely come to be.

This is your Primary Objective for the next week.

Take a moment and fill in the days of the week for the next week.

Go on to Day 50 and be amazing!

MY PRIMARY OBJECTIVE

_____

The most important thing I can do today to take me a step closer to my Primary Objective is _____.

The most important thing I can do today to take me a step closer to my Primary Objective is _____.

The most important thing I can do today to take me a step closer to my Primary Objective is _____.

The most important thing I can do today to take me a step closer to my Primary Objective is _____.

My new habit I'm developing (eliminating) is... _____

MORNING THOUGHTS AND INSPIRATIONS

My biggest frog to eat today...

_____

ACTION STEPS FOR TODAY

High Priority

1. _____

2. _____

3. _____

Medium Priority

1. _____

2. _____

3. _____

Low Priority

_____

_____

_____

_____

_____

_____

In which area(s) do I want to improve the most today?

Mental Health

Spiritual Health

Career Health

Physical Health

Social Health

Family Health

Financial Health

Weekly Goal Focus:

Today I am grateful for...

_____
_____
_____
_____
_____
_____
_____
_____
_____

How was my day? Did I feel good about my performance? What did I learn? Did I have a new insight? What would I do differently?

_____
_____
_____
_____
_____
_____
_____
_____

NOTES AND REFLECTIONS FROM TODAY

What was my energy level today? (lowest to highest) 1 2 3 4 5 6 7 8 9 10

If not a "10", what will I do tomorrow to make it closer to a "10"? _____

I ate my frog today: Yes   No

I did my new habit: Yes   No

What Time? _____

What Time? _____

"It does not matter how slowly you go as long as you do not stop."

Confucius

FOR TOMORROW

_____
_____
_____
_____

M T W T F S S

Date: _____

MY PRIMARY OBJECTIVE

The most important thing I can do today to take me a step closer to my Primary Objective is _____.

The most important thing I can do today to take me a step closer to my Primary Objective is _____.

The most important thing I can do today to take me a step closer to my Primary Objective is _____.

The most important thing I can do today to take me a step closer to my Primary Objective is _____.

My new habit I'm developing (eliminating) is... _____

MORNING THOUGHTS AND INSPIRATIONS

My biggest frog to eat today...

_____

ACTION STEPS FOR TODAY

High Priority

1. _____
2. _____
3. _____

Medium Priority

1. _____
2. _____
3. _____

Low Priority

_____
_____
_____
_____
_____
_____

In which area(s) do I want to improve the most today?

Mental Health

Spiritual Health

Career Health

Physical Health

Social Health

Family Health

Financial Health

Weekly Goal Focus:

Today I am grateful for...

_____
_____
_____
_____
_____
_____
_____
_____
_____

How was my day? Did I feel good about my performance? What did I learn? Did I have a new insight? What would I do differently?

_____
_____
_____
_____
_____
_____
_____

NOTES AND REFLECTIONS FROM TODAY

What was my energy level today? (lowest to highest) 1 2 3 4 5 6 7 8 9 10

If not a "10", what will I do tomorrow to make it closer to a "10"? _____

I ate my frog today: Yes   No

What Time? _____

I did my new habit: Yes   No

What Time? _____

FOR TOMORROW

_____
_____
_____
_____

"Follow your bliss and the universe will open doors for you where there were only walls."

Joseph Campbell

DAILY PREVIEW
DAY 52

M T W T F S S

Date: _____

MY PRIMARY OBJECTIVE

The most important thing I can do today to take me a step closer to my Primary Objective is _____.

The most important thing I can do today to take me a step closer to my Primary Objective is _____.

The most important thing I can do today to take me a step closer to my Primary Objective is _____.

The most important thing I can do today to take me a step closer to my Primary Objective is _____.

My new habit I'm developing (eliminating) is... _____

MORNING THOUGHTS AND INSPIRATIONS

My biggest frog to eat today...

_____

ACTION STEPS FOR TODAY

High Priority

1. _____
2. _____
3. _____

Medium Priority

1. _____
2. _____
3. _____

Low Priority

_____
_____
_____
_____
_____
_____

In which area(s) do I want to improve the most today?

Mental Health

Spiritual Health

Career Health

Physical Health

Social Health

Family Health

Financial Health

Weekly Goal Focus:

Today I am grateful for...

_____
_____
_____
_____
_____
_____
_____
_____
_____

How was my day? Did I feel good about my performance? What did I learn? Did I have a new insight? What would I do differently?

_____
_____
_____
_____
_____
_____
_____
_____

NOTES AND REFLECTIONS FROM TODAY

What was my energy level today? (lowest to highest) 1 2 3 4 5 6 7 8 9 10

If not a "10", what will I do tomorrow to make it closer to a "10"? _____

I ate my frog today: Yes   No

What Time? _____

I did my new habit: Yes   No

What Time? _____

"There are no traffic jams along the extra mile."

Roger Staubach

FOR TOMORROW

_____
_____
_____
_____

DAILY PREVIEW
DAY 53

M T W T F S S

Date: _____

MY PRIMARY OBJECTIVE

[_____]

The most important thing I can do today to take me a step closer to my Primary Objective is _____.

The most important thing I can do today to take me a step closer to my Primary Objective is _____.

The most important thing I can do today to take me a step closer to my Primary Objective is _____.

The most important thing I can do today to take me a step closer to my Primary Objective is _____.

My new habit I'm developing (eliminating) is... _____

MORNING THOUGHTS AND INSPIRATIONS

My biggest frog to eat today...

_____

ACTION STEPS FOR TODAY

High Priority
1. _____
2. _____
3. _____

Medium Priority
1. _____
2. _____
3. _____

Low Priority
_____
_____
_____
_____
_____
_____

In which area(s) do I want to improve the most today?

Mental Health

Spiritual Health

Career Health

Physical Health

Social Health

Family Health

Financial Health

Weekly Goal Focus:

Today I am grateful for...

_____
_____
_____
_____
_____
_____
_____
_____
_____

How was my day? Did I feel good about my performance? What did I learn? Did I have a new insight? What would I do differently?

_____
_____
_____
_____
_____
_____
_____

NOTES AND REFLECTIONS FROM TODAY

What was my energy level today? (lowest to highest) 1 2 3 4 5 6 7 8 9 10

If not a "10", what will I do tomorrow to make it closer to a "10"? _____

I ate my frog today: Yes No

What Time? _____

I did my new habit: Yes No

What Time? _____

FOR TOMORROW

_____
_____
_____
_____

"The battles that count aren't the ones for gold medals. The struggles within yourself—the invisible battles inside all of us—that's where it's at."

Jesse Owens

M T W T F S S

Date: _____

MY PRIMARY OBJECTIVE

The most important thing I can do today to take me a step closer to my Primary Objective is _____.

The most important thing I can do today to take me a step closer to my Primary Objective is _____.

The most important thing I can do today to take me a step closer to my Primary Objective is _____.

The most important thing I can do today to take me a step closer to my Primary Objective is _____.

My new habit I'm developing (eliminating) is... _____

MORNING THOUGHTS AND INSPIRATIONS

My biggest frog to eat today...

_____

ACTION STEPS FOR TODAY

High Priority
1. _____
2. _____
3. _____

Medium Priority
1. _____
2. _____
3. _____

Low Priority
_____
_____
_____
_____
_____
_____

In which area(s) do I want to improve the most today?

Mental Health

Spiritual Health

Career Health

Physical Health

Social Health

Family Health

Financial Health

Weekly Goal Focus:

Today I am grateful for...

_____
_____
_____
_____
_____
_____
_____
_____
_____
_____

How was my day? Did I feel good about my performance? What did I learn? Did I have a new insight? What would I do differently?

_____
_____
_____
_____
_____
_____
_____
_____
_____

NOTES AND REFLECTIONS FROM TODAY

What was my energy level today? (lowest to highest) 1 2 3 4 5 6 7 8 9 10

If not a "10", what will I do tomorrow to make it closer to a "10"? _____

I ate my frog today: Yes   No

I did my new habit: Yes   No

What Time? _____

What Time? _____

FOR TOMORROW

_____
_____
_____
_____

"Success seems to be largely a matter of hanging on after others have let go."

William Feather

DAILY PREVIEW
DAY 55

M T W T F S S

Date: _____

MY PRIMARY OBJECTIVE

[blank box]

The most important thing I can do today to take me a step closer to my Primary Objective is _____.

The most important thing I can do today to take me a step closer to my Primary Objective is _____.

The most important thing I can do today to take me a step closer to my Primary Objective is _____.

The most important thing I can do today to take me a step closer to my Primary Objective is _____.

My new habit I'm developing (eliminating) is... _____

MORNING THOUGHTS AND INSPIRATIONS

[blank box]

My biggest frog to eat today...

_____

ACTION STEPS FOR TODAY

High Priority

1. _____
2. _____
3. _____

Medium Priority

1. _____
2. _____
3. _____

Low Priority

_____
_____
_____
_____
_____
_____

In which area(s) do I want to improve the most today?

Mental Health

Spiritual Health

Career Health

Physical Health

Social Health

Family Health

Financial Health

Weekly Goal Focus:

Today I am grateful for...

_____
_____
_____
_____
_____
_____
_____
_____
_____

How was my day? Did I feel good about my performance? What did I learn? Did I have a new insight? What would I do differently?

_____
_____
_____
_____
_____
_____
_____
_____

NOTES AND REFLECTIONS FROM TODAY

What was my energy level today? (lowest to highest) 1 2 3 4 5 6 7 8 9 10

If not a "10", what will I do tomorrow to make it closer to a "10"? _____

I ate my frog today: Yes   No

What Time? _____

I did my new habit: Yes   No

What Time? _____

"Success is more a function of consistent common sense than it is of genius."

An Wang

FOR TOMORROW

_____
_____
_____
_____

DAILY PREVIEW
DAY 56

M T W T F S S

Date: _____

MY PRIMARY OBJECTIVE

[   ]

The most important thing I can do today to take me a step closer to my Primary Objective is _____.

The most important thing I can do today to take me a step closer to my Primary Objective is _____.

The most important thing I can do today to take me a step closer to my Primary Objective is _____.

The most important thing I can do today to take me a step closer to my Primary Objective is _____.

My new habit I'm developing (eliminating) is... _____

MORNING THOUGHTS AND INSPIRATIONS

My biggest frog to eat today...

_____

ACTION STEPS FOR TODAY

High Priority

1. _____
2. _____
3. _____

Medium Priority

1. _____
2. _____
3. _____

Low Priority

_____
_____
_____
_____
_____
_____

In which area(s) do I want to improve the most today?

Mental Health

Spiritual Health

Career Health

Physical Health

Social Health

Family Health

Financial Health

Weekly Goal Focus:

Today I am grateful for...

_____
_____
_____
_____
_____
_____
_____
_____

How was my day? Did I feel good about my performance? What did I learn? Did I have a new insight? What would I do differently?

_____
_____
_____
_____
_____
_____
_____
_____

NOTES AND REFLECTIONS FROM TODAY

What was my energy level today? (lowest to highest) 1 2 3 4 5 6 7 8 9 10

If not a "10", what will I do tomorrow to make it closer to a "10"? _____

I ate my frog today: Yes No

What Time? _____

I did my new habit: Yes No

What Time? _____

"Certain things catch your eye, but pursue only those that capture the heart."

Ancient Indian Proverb

FOR TOMORROW

_____
_____
_____
_____

WEEKLY CHECK-INS
WEEK 8

The Purpose of the Weekly Check-In is to...

1) Check-in with your progress throughout the week.

2) Re-focus for the upcoming week.

3) Get inspired for the future.

THE CHECK-IN

What have I accomplished since last week? What were the two most important things that I learned this week? Is there anything that I would have done differently? If so, what?

_____
_____
_____
_____
_____

What are my wins or victories since last week?

_____
_____
_____

What's the highlight (or low-light) of my week?

_____
_____
_____

What am I thankful for this week?

_____
_____
_____

The place I feel stuck is

_____
_____
_____

In which area(s) did I grow the most last week?

Mental Health

Spiritual Health

Career Health

Physical Health

Social Health

Family Health

Financial Health

What was my average energy level for the week?

1 2 3 4 5 6 7 8 9 10

What number do I want it to be next week?

1 2 3 4 5 6 7 8 9 10

How often did you eat your frog?

1 2 3 4 5 6 7

On a 1 - 10 scale, 1 being low and 10 being high, how grateful have I been feeling this last week?

1 2 3 4 5 6 7 8 9 10

How did I do with my new habit building/eliminating?

_____
_____
_____

Every week, we will be re-focusing on our future life. So, take a moment and fill this in again. There will be a few questions after you finish.

If there were no rules, and I could not fail, what would my life be like?

Describe your future life in detail and in writing...

_____
_____
_____
_____
_____
_____
_____

When you wrote this out again, how did you feel? Were you excited? Were you bored? Did your vision evolve? Was it different than before? Was there more detail or less? Did you even do this exercise? If not, how come?

_____
_____
_____

Look through your future life. Now, fill in the blank...

If I only accomplish _____ next week, my future life would surely come to be.

This is your Primary Objective for the next week.

Take a moment and fill in the days of the week for the next week.

Go on to Day 57 and be amazing!

M T W T F S S

Date: _____

MY PRIMARY OBJECTIVE

The most important thing I can do today to take me a step closer to my Primary Objective is _____.

The most important thing I can do today to take me a step closer to my Primary Objective is _____.

The most important thing I can do today to take me a step closer to my Primary Objective is _____.

The most important thing I can do today to take me a step closer to my Primary Objective is _____.

My new habit I'm developing (eliminating) is... _____

MORNING THOUGHTS AND INSPIRATIONS

My biggest frog to eat today...
_____

ACTION STEPS FOR TODAY

High Priority
1. _____
2. _____
3. _____

Medium Priority
1. _____
2. _____
3. _____

Low Priority
_____
_____
_____
_____
_____
_____

In which area(s) do I want to improve the most today?

Mental Health

Spiritual Health

Career Health

Physical Health

Social Health

Family Health

Financial Health

Today I am grateful for...

_____
_____
_____
_____
_____
_____
_____
_____
_____
_____

How was my day? Did I feel good about my performance? What did I learn? Did I have a new insight? What would I do differently?

_____
_____
_____
_____
_____
_____
_____
_____

NOTES AND REFLECTIONS FROM TODAY

What was my energy level today? (lowest to highest) 1 2 3 4 5 6 7 8 9 10

If not a "10", what will I do tomorrow to make it closer to a "10"? _____

I ate my frog today: Yes   No

What Time? _____

I did my new habit: Yes   No

What Time? _____

FOR TOMORROW

_____
_____
_____
_____

"Life is not measured by the number of breaths we take, but by the moments that take our breath away."

Maya Angelou

DAILY PREVIEW
DAY 58

M T W T F S S

Date: _____

MY PRIMARY OBJECTIVE

[blank box]

The most important thing I can do today to take me a step closer to my Primary Objective is _____.

The most important thing I can do today to take me a step closer to my Primary Objective is _____.

The most important thing I can do today to take me a step closer to my Primary Objective is _____.

The most important thing I can do today to take me a step closer to my Primary Objective is _____.

My new habit I'm developing (eliminating) is... _____

MORNING THOUGHTS AND INSPIRATIONS

My biggest frog to eat today...

_____

ACTION STEPS FOR TODAY

High Priority
1. _____
2. _____
3. _____

Medium Priority
1. _____
2. _____
3. _____

Low Priority
_____
_____
_____
_____
_____
_____

In which area(s) do I want to improve the most today?

Mental Health

Spiritual Health

Career Health

Physical Health

Social Health

Family Health

Financial Health

Weekly Goal Focus:

Today I am grateful for...

_____
_____
_____
_____
_____
_____
_____
_____

How was my day? Did I feel good about my performance? What did I learn? Did I have a new insight? What would I do differently?

_____
_____
_____
_____
_____
_____
_____
_____

NOTES AND REFLECTIONS FROM TODAY

What was my energy level today? (lowest to highest) 1 2 3 4 5 6 7 8 9 10

If not a "10", what will I do tomorrow to make it closer to a "10"? _____

I ate my frog today: Yes   No

What Time? _____

I did my new habit: Yes   No

What Time? _____

"When everything seems to be going against you, remember that the airplane takes off against the wind, not with it."

Henry Ford

FOR TOMORROW

_____
_____
_____
_____

M T W T F S S

Date: _____

MY PRIMARY OBJECTIVE

_____

The most important thing I can do today to take me a step closer to my Primary Objective is _____.

The most important thing I can do today to take me a step closer to my Primary Objective is _____.

The most important thing I can do today to take me a step closer to my Primary Objective is _____.

The most important thing I can do today to take me a step closer to my Primary Objective is _____.

My new habit I'm developing (eliminating) is... _____

MORNING THOUGHTS AND INSPIRATIONS

My biggest frog to eat today...

_____

ACTION STEPS FOR TODAY

High Priority

1. _____
2. _____
3. _____

Medium Priority

1. _____
2. _____
3. _____

Low Priority

_____
_____
_____
_____
_____
_____

In which area(s) do I want to improve the most today?

Mental Health

Spiritual Health

Career Health

Physical Health

Social Health

Family Health

Financial Health

Weekly Goal Focus:

Today I am grateful for...

_____
_____
_____
_____
_____
_____
_____
_____
_____

How was my day? Did I feel good about my performance? What did I learn? Did I have a new insight? What would I do differently?

_____
_____
_____
_____
_____
_____
_____
_____

NOTES AND REFLECTIONS FROM TODAY

What was my energy level today? (lowest to highest) 1 2 3 4 5 6 7 8 9 10

If not a "10", what will I do tomorrow to make it closer to a "10"? _____

I ate my frog today: Yes   No

What Time? _____

I did my new habit: Yes   No

What Time? _____

"Life is to be enjoyed, not endured"
Gordon B. Hinckley

FOR TOMORROW

_____
_____
_____
_____

M T W T F S S

Date: _____

MY PRIMARY OBJECTIVE

The most important thing I can do today to take me a step closer to my Primary Objective is _____.

The most important thing I can do today to take me a step closer to my Primary Objective is _____.

The most important thing I can do today to take me a step closer to my Primary Objective is _____.

The most important thing I can do today to take me a step closer to my Primary Objective is _____.

My new habit I'm developing (eliminating) is... _____

MORNING THOUGHTS AND INSPIRATIONS

My biggest frog to eat today...

_____

ACTION STEPS FOR TODAY

High Priority

1. _____
2. _____
3. _____

Medium Priority

1. _____
2. _____
3. _____

Low Priority

_____
_____
_____
_____
_____
_____

In which area(s) do I want to improve the most today?

Mental Health

Spiritual Health

Career Health

Physical Health

Social Health

Family Health

Financial Health

DAILY REVIEW
DAY 60

Today I am grateful for...

_____
_____
_____
_____
_____
_____
_____
_____
_____
_____

How was my day? Did I feel good about my performance? What did I learn? Did I have a new insight? What would I do differently?

_____
_____
_____
_____
_____
_____
_____
_____
_____

NOTES AND REFLECTIONS FROM TODAY

What was my energy level today? (lowest to highest) 1 2 3 4 5 6 7 8 9 10

If not a "10", what will I do tomorrow to make it closer to a "10"? _____

I ate my frog today: Yes   No

What Time? _____

I did my new habit: Yes   No

What Time? _____

"We must believe that we are gifted for something, and that this thing, at whatever cost, must be attained."

Marie Curie

FOR TOMORROW

_____
_____
_____
_____

DAILY PREVIEW
DAY 61

M T W T F S S

Date: _____

MY PRIMARY OBJECTIVE

The most important thing I can do today to take me a step closer to my Primary Objective is _____.

The most important thing I can do today to take me a step closer to my Primary Objective is _____.

The most important thing I can do today to take me a step closer to my Primary Objective is _____.

The most important thing I can do today to take me a step closer to my Primary Objective is _____.

My new habit I'm developing (eliminating) is... _____

MORNING THOUGHTS AND INSPIRATIONS

My biggest frog to eat today...

_____

ACTION STEPS FOR TODAY

High Priority

1. _____
2. _____
3. _____

Medium Priority

1. _____
2. _____
3. _____

Low Priority

_____
_____
_____
_____
_____
_____

In which area(s) do I want to improve the most today?

Mental Health

Spiritual Health

Career Health

Physical Health

Social Health

Family Health

Financial Health

Today I am grateful for...

_____
_____
_____
_____
_____
_____
_____
_____
_____

How was my day? Did I feel good about my performance? What did I learn? Did I have a new insight? What would I do differently?

_____
_____
_____
_____
_____
_____
_____
_____

NOTES AND REFLECTIONS FROM TODAY

What was my energy level today? (lowest to highest) 1 2 3 4 5 6 7 8 9 10

If not a "10", what will I do tomorrow to make it closer to a "10"? _____

I ate my frog today: Yes   No

What Time? _____

I did my new habit: Yes   No

What Time? _____

"Life can only be understood backwards; but it must be lived forwards."

Søren Kierkegaard

FOR TOMORROW

_____
_____
_____
_____

DAILY PREVIEW
DAY 62

M T W T F S S

Date: _____

MY PRIMARY OBJECTIVE 👉 [   ]

The most important thing I can do today to take me a step closer to my Primary Objective is _____.

The most important thing I can do today to take me a step closer to my Primary Objective is _____.

The most important thing I can do today to take me a step closer to my Primary Objective is _____.

The most important thing I can do today to take me a step closer to my Primary Objective is _____.

My new habit I'm developing (eliminating) is... _____

MORNING THOUGHTS AND INSPIRATIONS

My biggest frog to eat today...
_____

ACTION STEPS FOR TODAY

High Priority
1. _____
2. _____
3. _____

Medium Priority
1. _____
2. _____
3. _____

Low Priority
_____
_____
_____
_____
_____
_____

In which area(s) do I want to improve the most today?

Mental Health

Spiritual Health

Career Health

Physical Health

Social Health

Family Health

Financial Health

Weekly Goal Focus:

Today I am grateful for...

_____
_____
_____
_____
_____
_____
_____
_____
_____
_____

How was my day? Did I feel good about my performance? What did I learn? Did I have a new insight? What would I do differently?

_____
_____
_____
_____
_____
_____
_____
_____

NOTES AND REFLECTIONS FROM TODAY

What was my energy level today? (lowest to highest) 1 2 3 4 5 6 7 8 9 10

If not a "10", what will I do tomorrow to make it closer to a "10"? _____

I ate my frog today: Yes   No

What Time? _____

I did my new habit: Yes   No

What Time? _____

"Get busy living or get busy dying."

Stephen King

FOR TOMORROW

_____
_____
_____
_____

DAILY PREVIEW
DAY 63

M T W T F S S

Date: _____

MY PRIMARY OBJECTIVE

☞ [ ]

The most important thing I can do today to take me a step closer to my Primary Objective is _____.

The most important thing I can do today to take me a step closer to my Primary Objective is _____.

The most important thing I can do today to take me a step closer to my Primary Objective is _____.

The most important thing I can do today to take me a step closer to my Primary Objective is _____.

My new habit I'm developing (eliminating) is... _____

MORNING THOUGHTS AND INSPIRATIONS ☀

[ ]

My biggest frog to eat today...

_____

ACTION STEPS FOR TODAY ⚑

High Priority

1. _____
2. _____
3. _____

Medium Priority

1. _____
2. _____
3. _____

Low Priority

_____
_____
_____
_____
_____
_____

In which area(s) do I want to improve the most today?

Mental Health

Spiritual Health

Career Health

Physical Health

Social Health

Family Health

Financial Health

Weekly Goal Focus:

Today I am grateful for...

_____
_____
_____
_____
_____
_____
_____
_____
_____

How was my day? Did I feel good about my performance? What did I learn? Did I have a new insight? What would I do differently?

_____
_____
_____
_____
_____
_____
_____
_____

NOTES AND REFLECTIONS FROM TODAY

What was my energy level today? (lowest to highest) 1 2 3 4 5 6 7 8 9 10

If not a "10", what will I do tomorrow to make it closer to a "10"? _____

I ate my frog today: Yes   No

What Time? _____

I did my new habit: Yes   No

What Time? _____

"Life is like a novel. It's filled with suspense. You have no idea what is going to happen until you turn the page."

Sidney Sheldon J

FOR TOMORROW

_____
_____
_____
_____

WEEKLY CHECK-INS
WEEK 9

The Purpose of the Weekly Check-In is to...

1) Check-in with your progress throughout the week.

2) Re-focus for the upcoming week.

3) Get inspired for the future.

THE CHECK-IN

What have I accomplished since last week? What were the two most important things that I learned this week? Is there anything that I would have done differently? If so, what?

_____
_____
_____
_____
_____

What are my wins or victories since last week?

_____
_____
_____

What's the highlight (or low-light) of my week?

_____
_____
_____

What am I thankful for this week?

_____
_____
_____

The place I feel stuck is

_____
_____
_____

In which area(s) did I grow the most last week?

Mental Health

Spiritual Health

Career Health

Physical Health

Social Health

Family Health

Financial Health

What was my average energy level for the week?

1 2 3 4 5 6 7 8 9 10

What number do I want it to be next week?

1 2 3 4 5 6 7 8 9 10

How often did you eat your frog?

1 2 3 4 5 6 7

On a 1 - 10 scale, 1 being low and 10 being high, how grateful have I been feeling this last week?

1 2 3 4 5 6 7 8 9 10

How did I do with my new habit building/eliminating?

_____
_____
_____

Every week, we will be re-focusing on our future life. So, take a moment and fill this in again. There will be a few questions after you finish.

If there were no rules, and I could not fail, what would my life be like?

Describe your future life in detail and in writing...

_____

_____

_____

_____

_____

_____

_____

When you wrote this out again, how did you feel? Were you excited? Were you bored? Did your vision evolve? Was it different than before? Was there more detail or less? Did you even do this exercise? If not, how come?

_____

_____

_____

Look through your future life. Now, fill in the blank...

If I only accomplish _____ next week, my future life would surely come to be.

This is your Primary Objective for the next week.

Take a moment and fill in the days of the week for the next week.

Go on to Day 64 and be amazing!

DAILY PREVIEW
DAY 64

M T W T F S S

Date: _____

MY PRIMARY OBJECTIVE

The most important thing I can do today to take me a step closer to my Primary Objective is _____.

The most important thing I can do today to take me a step closer to my Primary Objective is _____.

The most important thing I can do today to take me a step closer to my Primary Objective is _____.

The most important thing I can do today to take me a step closer to my Primary Objective is _____.

My new habit I'm developing (eliminating) is... _____

MORNING THOUGHTS AND INSPIRATIONS

My biggest frog to eat today...

_____

ACTION STEPS FOR TODAY

High Priority

1. _____

2. _____

3. _____

Medium Priority

1. _____

2. _____

3. _____

Low Priority

_____

_____

_____

_____

_____

_____

In which area(s) do I want to improve the most today?

Mental Health

Spiritual Health

Career Health

Physical Health

Social Health

Family Health

Financial Health

Weekly Goal Focus:

Today I am grateful for...

_____
_____
_____
_____
_____
_____
_____
_____
_____

How was my day? Did I feel good about my performance? What did I learn? Did I have a new insight? What would I do differently?

_____
_____
_____
_____
_____
_____
_____
_____

NOTES AND REFLECTIONS FROM TODAY

What was my energy level today? (lowest to highest) 1 2 3 4 5 6 7 8 9 10

If not a "10", what will I do tomorrow to make it closer to a "10"? _____

I ate my frog today: Yes   No

What Time? _____

I did my new habit: Yes   No

What Time? _____

"The more you praise and celebrate your life, the more there is in life to celebrate."

Oprah Winfrey

FOR TOMORROW

_____
_____
_____
_____

DAILY PREVIEW
DAY 65

M T W T F S S

Date: _____

MY PRIMARY OBJECTIVE

[ ]

The most important thing I can do today to take me a step closer to my Primary Objective is _____ .

The most important thing I can do today to take me a step closer to my Primary Objective is _____ .

The most important thing I can do today to take me a step closer to my Primary Objective is _____ .

The most important thing I can do today to take me a step closer to my Primary Objective is _____ .

My new habit I'm developing (eliminating) is... _____

MORNING THOUGHTS AND INSPIRATIONS

My biggest frog to eat today...

_____

ACTION STEPS FOR TODAY

High Priority
1. _____
2. _____
3. _____

Medium Priority
1. _____
2. _____
3. _____

Low Priority
_____
_____
_____
_____
_____
_____

In which area(s) do I want to improve the most today?

Mental Health

Spiritual Health

Career Health

Physical Health

Social Health

Family Health

Financial Health

Today I am grateful for...

_____
_____
_____
_____
_____
_____
_____
_____
_____

How was my day? Did I feel good about my performance? What did I learn? Did I have a new insight? What would I do differently?

_____
_____
_____
_____
_____
_____
_____
_____

NOTES AND REFLECTIONS FROM TODAY

What was my energy level today? (lowest to highest)   1 2 3 4 5 6 7 8 9 10

If not a "10", what will I do tomorrow to make it closer to a "10"? _____

I ate my frog today: Yes   No

What Time? _____

I did my new habit: Yes   No

What Time? _____

FOR TOMORROW

_____
_____
_____
_____

"Life isn't as serious as the mind makes it out to be."

Eckhart Tolle

DAILY PREVIEW
DAY 66

M T W T F S S

Date: _____

MY PRIMARY OBJECTIVE

[_____]

The most important thing I can do today to take me a step closer to my Primary Objective is _____.

The most important thing I can do today to take me a step closer to my Primary Objective is _____.

The most important thing I can do today to take me a step closer to my Primary Objective is _____.

The most important thing I can do today to take me a step closer to my Primary Objective is _____.

My new habit I'm developing (eliminating) is... _____

MORNING THOUGHTS AND INSPIRATIONS

My biggest frog to eat today...

_____

ACTION STEPS FOR TODAY

High Priority

1. _____
2. _____
3. _____

Medium Priority

1. _____
2. _____
3. _____

Low Priority

_____
_____
_____
_____
_____
_____

In which area(s) do I want to improve the most today?

Mental Health

Spiritual Health

Career Health

Physical Health

Social Health

Family Health

Financial Health

Weekly Goal Focus:

Today I am grateful for...

_____
_____
_____
_____
_____
_____
_____
_____

How was my day? Did I feel good about my performance? What did I learn? Did I have a new insight? What would I do differently?

_____
_____
_____
_____
_____
_____
_____
_____

NOTES AND REFLECTIONS FROM TODAY

What was my energy level today? (lowest to highest) 1 2 3 4 5 6 7 8 9 10

If not a "10", what will I do tomorrow to make it closer to a "10"? _____

I ate my frog today: Yes No

What Time? _____

I did my new habit: Yes No

What Time? _____

"A fit, healthy body—that is the best fashion statement"

Jess C. Scott

FOR TOMORROW

_____
_____
_____
_____

DAILY PREVIEW
DAY 67

M T W T F S S

Date: _____

MY PRIMARY OBJECTIVE 👆

[   ]

The most important thing I can do today to take me a step closer to my Primary Objective is _____.

The most important thing I can do today to take me a step closer to my Primary Objective is _____.

The most important thing I can do today to take me a step closer to my Primary Objective is _____.

The most important thing I can do today to take me a step closer to my Primary Objective is _____.

My new habit I'm developing (eliminating) is... _____

MORNING THOUGHTS AND INSPIRATIONS ☀

[   ]

My biggest frog to eat today...

_____

ACTION STEPS FOR TODAY 🏳

High Priority

1. _____
2. _____
3. _____

Medium Priority

1. _____
2. _____
3. _____

Low Priority

_____
_____
_____
_____
_____
_____

In which area(s) do I want to improve the most today?

Mental Health

Spiritual Health

Career Health

Physical Health

Social Health

Family Health

Financial Health

Weekly Goal Focus:

Today I am grateful for...

_____
_____
_____
_____
_____
_____
_____
_____
_____

How was my day? Did I feel good about my performance? What did I learn? Did I have a new insight? What would I do differently?

_____
_____
_____
_____
_____
_____
_____
_____

NOTES AND REFLECTIONS FROM TODAY

What was my energy level today? (lowest to highest) 1 2 3 4 5 6 7 8 9 10

If not a "10", what will I do tomorrow to make it closer to a "10"? _____

I ate my frog today: Yes   No

What Time? _____

I did my new habit: Yes   No

What Time? _____

"Either you run the day, or the day runs you."

Jim Rohn

FOR TOMORROW

_____
_____
_____
_____

DAILY PREVIEW
DAY 68

M T W T F S S

Date: _____

MY PRIMARY OBJECTIVE

[   ]

The most important thing I can do today to take me a step closer to my Primary Objective is _____.

The most important thing I can do today to take me a step closer to my Primary Objective is _____.

The most important thing I can do today to take me a step closer to my Primary Objective is _____.

The most important thing I can do today to take me a step closer to my Primary Objective is _____.

My new habit I'm developing (eliminating) is... _____

MORNING THOUGHTS AND INSPIRATIONS

My biggest frog to eat today...

_____

ACTION STEPS FOR TODAY

High Priority
1. _____
2. _____
3. _____

Medium Priority
1. _____
2. _____
3. _____

Low Priority
_____
_____
_____
_____
_____
_____

In which area(s) do I want to improve the most today?

Mental Health

Spiritual Health

Career Health

Physical Health

Social Health

Family Health

Financial Health

Weekly Goal Focus:

Today I am grateful for...

_____
_____
_____
_____
_____
_____
_____
_____
_____

How was my day? Did I feel good about my performance? What did I learn? Did I have a new insight? What would I do differently?

_____
_____
_____
_____
_____
_____
_____
_____

NOTES AND REFLECTIONS FROM TODAY

What was my energy level today? (lowest to highest) 1 2 3 4 5 6 7 8 9 10

If not a "10", what will I do tomorrow to make it closer to a "10"? _____

I ate my frog today: Yes   No

What Time? _____

I did my new habit: Yes   No

What Time? _____

FOR TOMORROW

_____
_____
_____
_____

"Here is a test to find out whether your mission in life is complete. If You're still alive, it isn't."

Lauren Bacall

DAILY PREVIEW
DAY 69

M T W T F S S

Date: _____

MY PRIMARY OBJECTIVE ☞

[   ]

My biggest frog to eat today...

_____

ACTION STEPS FOR TODAY ⚑

The most important thing I can do today to take me a step closer to my Primary Objective is _____.

The most important thing I can do today to take me a step closer to my Primary Objective is _____.

The most important thing I can do today to take me a step closer to my Primary Objective is _____.

The most important thing I can do today to take me a step closer to my Primary Objective is _____.

My new habit I'm developing (eliminating) is... _____

MORNING THOUGHTS AND INSPIRATIONS ☀

High Priority
1. _____
2. _____
3. _____

Medium Priority
1. _____
2. _____
3. _____

Low Priority
_____
_____
_____
_____
_____
_____
_____

In which area(s) do I want to improve the most today?

Mental Health

Spiritual Health

Career Health

Physical Health

Social Health

Family Health

Financial Health

Weekly Goal Focus:

Today I am grateful for...

_____
_____
_____
_____
_____
_____
_____
_____
_____

How was my day? Did I feel good about my performance? What did I learn? Did I have a new insight? What would I do differently?

_____
_____
_____
_____
_____
_____
_____
_____

NOTES AND REFLECTIONS FROM TODAY

What was my energy level today? (lowest to highest) 1 2 3 4 5 6 7 8 9 10

If not a "10", what will I do tomorrow to make it closer to a "10"? _____

I ate my frog today: Yes No

What Time? _____

I did my new habit: Yes No

What Time? _____

FOR TOMORROW

_____
_____
_____
_____

"Life is like riding a bicycle. To keep your balance, you must keep moving."
Albert Einstein

DAILY PREVIEW
DAY 70

M T W T F S S

Date: _____

MY PRIMARY OBJECTIVE

The most important thing I can do today to take me a step closer to my Primary Objective is _____.

The most important thing I can do today to take me a step closer to my Primary Objective is _____.

The most important thing I can do today to take me a step closer to my Primary Objective is _____.

The most important thing I can do today to take me a step closer to my Primary Objective is _____.

My new habit I'm developing (eliminating) is... _____

MORNING THOUGHTS AND INSPIRATIONS

My biggest frog to eat today...

_____

ACTION STEPS FOR TODAY

High Priority

1. _____
2. _____
3. _____

Medium Priority

1. _____
2. _____
3. _____

Low Priority

_____
_____
_____
_____
_____
_____

In which area(s) do I want to improve the most today?

Mental Health

Spiritual Health

Career Health

Physical Health

Social Health

Family Health

Financial Health

Weekly Goal Focus:

Today I am grateful for...

_____

_____

_____

_____

_____

_____

_____

_____

How was my day? Did I feel good about my performance? What did I learn? Did I have a new insight? What would I do differently?

_____

_____

_____

_____

_____

_____

_____

_____

_____

NOTES AND REFLECTIONS FROM TODAY

What was my energy level today? (lowest to highest) 1 2 3 4 5 6 7 8 9 10

If not a "10", what will I do tomorrow to make it closer to a "10"? _____

I ate my frog today: Yes   No

What Time? _____

I did my new habit: Yes   No

What Time? _____

"Little by little, a little becomes a lot."

Tanzanian Proverb

FOR TOMORROW

_____

_____

_____

_____

WEEKLY CHECK-INS
WEEK 10

The Purpose of the Weekly Check-In is to...

1) *Check-in with your progress throughout the week.*

2) *Re-focus for the upcoming week.*

3) *Get inspired for the future.*

THE CHECK-IN

What have I accomplished since last week? What were the two most important things that I learned this week? Is there anything that I would have done differently? If so, what?

_____

_____

_____

_____

_____

What are my wins or victories since last week?

_____

_____

_____

What's the highlight (or low-light) of my week?

_____

_____

_____

What am I thankful for this week?

_____

_____

_____

The place I feel stuck is

_____

_____

_____

In which area(s) did I grow the most last week?

Mental Health

Spiritual Health

Career Health

Physical Health

Social Health

Family Health

Financial Health

What was my average energy level for the week?

1 2 3 4 5 6 7 8 9 10

What number do I want it to be next week?

1 2 3 4 5 6 7 8 9 10

How often did you eat your frog?

1 2 3 4 5 6 7

On a 1 - 10 scale, 1 being low and 10 being high, how grateful have I been feeling this last week?

1 2 3 4 5 6 7 8 9 10

How did I do with my new habit building/eliminating?

_____

_____

_____

Every week, we will be re-focusing on our future life. So, take a moment and fill this in again. There will be a few questions after you finish.

RE-FOCUS
WEEK 10

If there were no rules, and I could not fail, what would my life be like?

Describe your future life in detail and in writing...

_____

_____

_____

_____

_____

_____

_____

When you wrote this out again, how did you feel? Were you excited? Were you bored? Did your vision evolve? Was it different than before? Was there more detail or less? Did you even do this exercise? If not, how come?

_____

_____

_____

Look through your future life. Now, fill in the blank...

If I only accomplish _____ next week, my future life would surely come to be.

This is your Primary Objective for the next week.

Take a moment and fill in the days of the week for the next week.

Go on to Day 71 and be amazing!

DAILY PREVIEW
DAY 71

M T W T F S S

Date: _____

MY PRIMARY OBJECTIVE 👉 [_____]

The most important thing I can do today to take me a step closer to my Primary Objective is _____.

The most important thing I can do today to take me a step closer to my Primary Objective is _____.

The most important thing I can do today to take me a step closer to my Primary Objective is _____.

The most important thing I can do today to take me a step closer to my Primary Objective is _____.

My new habit I'm developing (eliminating) is... _____

MORNING THOUGHTS AND INSPIRATIONS ☀

My biggest frog to eat today...
_____

ACTION STEPS FOR TODAY ⚑

High Priority
1. _____
2. _____
3. _____

Medium Priority
1. _____
2. _____
3. _____

Low Priority
_____
_____
_____
_____
_____
_____

In which area(s) do I want to improve the most today?

Mental Health

Spiritual Health

Career Health

Physical Health

Social Health

Family Health

Financial Health

Today I am grateful for...

_____
_____
_____
_____
_____
_____
_____
_____
_____

How was my day? Did I feel good about my performance? What did I learn? Did I have a new insight? What would I do differently?

_____
_____
_____
_____
_____
_____
_____
_____

NOTES AND REFLECTIONS FROM TODAY

What was my energy level today? (lowest to highest) 1 2 3 4 5 6 7 8 9 10

If not a "10", what will I do tomorrow to make it closer to a "10"? _____

I ate my frog today: Yes   No

What Time? _____

I did my new habit: Yes   No

What Time? _____

"Do not go where the path may lead, go instead where there is no path and leave a trail."

Ralph Waldo Emerson

FOR TOMORROW

_____
_____
_____
_____

M T W T F S S

Date: _____

My biggest frog to eat today...

_____

ACTION STEPS
FOR TODAY

MY PRIMARY
OBJECTIVE

[ ]

The most important thing I can do today to take me a step closer to my Primary Objective is _____.

The most important thing I can do today to take me a step closer to my Primary Objective is _____.

The most important thing I can do today to take me a step closer to my Primary Objective is _____.

The most important thing I can do today to take me a step closer to my Primary Objective is _____.

My new habit I'm developing (eliminating) is... _____

MORNING
THOUGHTS
AND INSPIRATIONS

High Priority

1. _____
2. _____
3. _____

Medium Priority

1. _____
2. _____
3. _____

Low Priority

_____
_____
_____
_____
_____
_____

In which area(s) do I want to improve the most today?

Mental Health

Spiritual Health

Career Health

Physical Health

Social Health

Family Health

Financial Health

Today I am grateful for...

_____
_____
_____
_____
_____
_____
_____
_____
_____

How was my day? Did I feel good about my performance? What did I learn? Did I have a new insight? What would I do differently?

_____
_____
_____
_____
_____
_____
_____
_____

NOTES AND REFLECTIONS FROM TODAY

What was my energy level today? (lowest to highest) 1 2 3 4 5 6 7 8 9 10

If not a "10", what will I do tomorrow to make it closer to a "10"? _____

I ate my frog today: Yes   No

What Time? _____

I did my new habit: Yes   No

What Time? _____

"Be happy, but never satisfied."

Bruce Lee

FOR TOMORROW

_____
_____
_____
_____

DAILY PREVIEW
DAY 73

M T W T F S S

Date: _____

MY PRIMARY OBJECTIVE

The most important thing I can do today to take me a step closer to my Primary Objective is _____.

The most important thing I can do today to take me a step closer to my Primary Objective is _____.

The most important thing I can do today to take me a step closer to my Primary Objective is _____.

The most important thing I can do today to take me a step closer to my Primary Objective is _____.

My new habit I'm developing (eliminating) is... _____

MORNING THOUGHTS AND INSPIRATIONS

My biggest frog to eat today...

_____

ACTION STEPS FOR TODAY

High Priority

1. _____
2. _____
3. _____

Medium Priority

1. _____
2. _____
3. _____

Low Priority

_____
_____
_____
_____
_____
_____

In which area(s) do I want to improve the most today?

Mental Health

Spiritual Health

Career Health

Physical Health

Social Health

Family Health

Financial Health

Weekly Goal Focus:

Today I am grateful for...

_____
_____
_____
_____
_____
_____
_____
_____

How was my day? Did I feel good about my performance? What did I learn? Did I have a new insight? What would I do differently?

_____
_____
_____
_____
_____
_____
_____
_____

NOTES AND REFLECTIONS FROM TODAY

What was my energy level today? (lowest to highest) 1 2 3 4 5 6 7 8 9 10

If not a "10", what will I do tomorrow to make it closer to a "10"? _____

I ate my frog today: Yes   No

What Time? _____

I did my new habit: Yes   No

What Time? _____

FOR TOMORROW

_____
_____
_____
_____

"It doesn't matter where you are coming from. All that matters is where you are going."

Brian Tracy

M T W T F S S

Date: _____

MY PRIMARY OBJECTIVE 👆 [   ]

The most important thing I can do today to take me a step closer to my Primary Objective is _____.

The most important thing I can do today to take me a step closer to my Primary Objective is _____.

The most important thing I can do today to take me a step closer to my Primary Objective is _____.

The most important thing I can do today to take me a step closer to my Primary Objective is _____.

My new habit I'm developing (eliminating) is... _____

MORNING THOUGHTS AND INSPIRATIONS ☀

My biggest frog to eat today...

_____

ACTION STEPS FOR TODAY 🚩

High Priority

1. _____
2. _____
3. _____

Medium Priority

1. _____
2. _____
3. _____

Low Priority

_____
_____
_____
_____
_____
_____

In which area(s) do I want to improve the most today?

Mental Health

Spiritual Health

Career Health

Physical Health

Social Health

Family Health

Financial Health

Weekly Goal Focus:

Today I am grateful for...

_____

_____

_____

_____

_____

_____

_____

_____

_____

How was my day? Did I feel good about my performance? What did I learn? Did I have a new insight? What would I do differently?

_____

_____

_____

_____

_____

_____

_____

_____

NOTES AND REFLECTIONS FROM TODAY

What was my energy level today? (lowest to highest) 1 2 3 4 5 6 7 8 9 10

If not a "10", what will I do tomorrow to make it closer to a "10"? _____

I ate my frog today: Yes   No

What Time? _____

I did my new habit: Yes   No

What Time? _____

FOR TOMORROW

_____

_____

_____

_____

"The aim of life is self-development. To realize one's nature perfectly - that is what each of us is here for."

Oscar Wilde

DAILY PREVIEW
DAY 75

M T W T F S S

Date: _____

MY PRIMARY OBJECTIVE ☝

[ ]

The most important thing I can do today to take me a step closer to my Primary Objective is _____.

The most important thing I can do today to take me a step closer to my Primary Objective is _____.

The most important thing I can do today to take me a step closer to my Primary Objective is _____.

The most important thing I can do today to take me a step closer to my Primary Objective is _____.

My new habit I'm developing (eliminating) is... _____

MORNING THOUGHTS AND INSPIRATIONS ☀

My biggest frog to eat today...
_____

ACTION STEPS FOR TODAY ⚑

High Priority
1. _____
2. _____
3. _____

Medium Priority
1. _____
2. _____
3. _____

Low Priority
_____
_____
_____
_____
_____
_____

In which area(s) do I want to improve the most today?

Mental Health

Spiritual Health

Career Health

Physical Health

Social Health

Family Health

Financial Health

Today I am grateful for...

_____
_____
_____
_____
_____
_____
_____
_____
_____
_____

How was my day? Did I feel good about my performance? What did I learn? Did I have a new insight? What would I do differently?

_____
_____
_____
_____
_____
_____
_____
_____
_____

NOTES AND REFLECTIONS FROM TODAY

What was my energy level today? (lowest to highest) 1 2 3 4 5 6 7 8 9 10

If not a "10", what will I do tomorrow to make it closer to a "10"? _____

I ate my frog today: Yes No

What Time? _____

I did my new habit: Yes No

What Time? _____

"How wonderful it is that nobody need wait a single moment before starting to improve the world."

Anne Frank

FOR TOMORROW

_____
_____
_____
_____

M T W T F S S

Date: _____

MY PRIMARY OBJECTIVE

☞

The most important thing I can do today to take me a step closer to my Primary Objective is _____.

The most important thing I can do today to take me a step closer to my Primary Objective is _____.

The most important thing I can do today to take me a step closer to my Primary Objective is _____.

The most important thing I can do today to take me a step closer to my Primary Objective is _____.

My new habit I'm developing (eliminating) is... _____

MORNING THOUGHTS AND INSPIRATIONS

My biggest frog to eat today...

_____

ACTION STEPS FOR TODAY

High Priority

1. _____
2. _____
3. _____

Medium Priority

1. _____
2. _____
3. _____

Low Priority

_____
_____
_____
_____
_____
_____

In which area(s) do I want to improve the most today?

Mental Health

Spiritual Health

Career Health

Physical Health

Social Health

Family Health

Financial Health

Weekly Goal Focus:

Today I am grateful for...

_____
_____
_____
_____
_____
_____
_____
_____
_____

How was my day? Did I feel good about my performance? What did I learn? Did I have a new insight? What would I do differently?

_____
_____
_____
_____
_____
_____
_____
_____

NOTES AND REFLECTIONS FROM TODAY

What was my energy level today? (lowest to highest) 1 2 3 4 5 6 7 8 9 10

If not a "10", what will I do tomorrow to make it closer to a "10"? _____

I ate my frog today: Yes   No

What Time? _____

I did my new habit: Yes   No

What Time? _____

"If you don't know where you're going, any road'll take you there"

Geoge Harrison

FOR TOMORROW

_____
_____
_____
_____

M T W T F S S

Date: _____

My biggest frog to eat today...

_____

ACTION STEPS FOR TODAY

MY PRIMARY OBJECTIVE

[_____]

The most important thing I can do today to take me a step closer to my Primary Objective is _____.

The most important thing I can do today to take me a step closer to my Primary Objective is _____.

The most important thing I can do today to take me a step closer to my Primary Objective is _____.

The most important thing I can do today to take me a step closer to my Primary Objective is _____.

My new habit I'm developing (eliminating) is... _____

High Priority

1. _____
2. _____
3. _____

Medium Priority

1. _____
2. _____
3. _____

Low Priority

_____
_____
_____
_____
_____
_____

MORNING THOUGHTS AND INSPIRATIONS

In which area(s) do I want to improve the most today?

Mental Health

Spiritual Health

Career Health

Physical Health

Social Health

Family Health

Financial Health

Weekly Goal Focus:

Today I am grateful for...

_____
_____
_____
_____
_____
_____
_____
_____

How was my day? Did I feel good about my performance? What did I learn? Did I have a new insight? What would I do differently?

_____
_____
_____
_____
_____
_____
_____
_____

NOTES AND REFLECTIONS FROM TODAY

What was my energy level today? (lowest to highest) 1 2 3 4 5 6 7 8 9 10

If not a "10", what will I do tomorrow to make it closer to a "10"? _____

I ate my frog today: Yes   No

What Time? _____

I did my new habit: Yes   No

What Time? _____

"Everything you can imagine is real."

Pablo Picasso

FOR TOMORROW

_____
_____
_____
_____

WEEKLY CHECK-INS
WEEK 11

The Purpose of the Weekly Check-In is to...

1) Check-in with your progress throughout the week.

2) Re-focus for the upcoming week.

3) Get inspired for the future.

THE CHECK-IN

What have I accomplished since last week? What were the two most important things that I learned this week? Is there anything that I would have done differently? If so, what?

_____
_____
_____
_____
_____

What are my wins or victories since last week?

_____
_____
_____

What's the highlight (or low-light) of my week?

_____
_____
_____

What am I thankful for this week?

_____
_____
_____

The place I feel stuck is

_____
_____
_____

In which area(s) did I grow the most last week?

Mental Health

Spiritual Health

Career Health

Physical Health

Social Health

Family Health

Financial Health

What was my average energy level for the week?

1 2 3 4 5 6 7 8 9 10

What number do I want it to be next week?

1 2 3 4 5 6 7 8 9 10

How often did you eat your frog?

1 2 3 4 5 6 7

On a 1 - 10 scale, 1 being low and 10 being high, how grateful have I been feeling this last week?

1 2 3 4 5 6 7 8 9 10

How did I do with my new habit building/eliminating?

_____
_____
_____

Every week, we will be re-focusing on our future life. So, take a moment and fill this in again. There will be a few questions after you finish.

If there were no rules, and I could not fail, what would my life be like?

Describe your future life in detail and in writing...

_____

_____

_____

_____

_____

_____

_____

When you wrote this out again, how did you feel? Were you excited? Were you bored? Did your vision evolve? Was it different than before? Was there more detail or less? Did you even do this exercise? If not, how come?

_____

_____

_____

Look through your future life. Now, fill in the blank...

If I only accomplish _____ next week, my future life would surely come to be.

This is your Primary Objective for the next week.

Take a moment and fill in the days of the week for the next week.

Go on to Day 78 and be amazing!

DAILY PREVIEW
DAY 78

M T W T F S S

Date: _____

MY PRIMARY OBJECTIVE

[_____]

The most important thing I can do today to take me a step closer to my Primary Objective is _____.

The most important thing I can do today to take me a step closer to my Primary Objective is _____.

The most important thing I can do today to take me a step closer to my Primary Objective is _____.

The most important thing I can do today to take me a step closer to my Primary Objective is _____.

My new habit I'm developing (eliminating) is... _____

MORNING THOUGHTS AND INSPIRATIONS

My biggest frog to eat today...

_____

ACTION STEPS FOR TODAY

High Priority

1. _____
2. _____
3. _____

Medium Priority

1. _____
2. _____
3. _____

Low Priority

_____
_____
_____
_____
_____
_____

In which area(s) do I want to improve the most today?

Mental Health

Spiritual Health

Career Health

Physical Health

Social Health

Family Health

Financial Health

Weekly Goal Focus:

Today I am grateful for...

_____
_____
_____
_____
_____
_____
_____
_____
_____

How was my day? Did I feel good about my performance? What did I learn? Did I have a new insight? What would I do differently?

_____
_____
_____
_____
_____
_____
_____
_____
_____

NOTES AND REFLECTIONS FROM TODAY

What was my energy level today? (lowest to highest) 1 2 3 4 5 6 7 8 9 10

If not a "10", what will I do tomorrow to make it closer to a "10"? _____

I ate my frog today: Yes   No

What Time? _____

I did my new habit: Yes   No

What Time? _____

FOR TOMORROW

_____
_____
_____
_____

"Listen to the mustn'ts, child. Listen to the don'ts. Listen to the shouldn'ts, the impossibles, the won'ts. Listen to the never haves, then listen close to me... Anything can happen, child. Anything can be."

Shel Silverstein

M T W T F S S

Date: _____

My biggest frog to eat today...

_____

MY PRIMARY OBJECTIVE

The most important thing I can do today to take me a step closer to my Primary Objective is _____.

The most important thing I can do today to take me a step closer to my Primary Objective is _____.

The most important thing I can do today to take me a step closer to my Primary Objective is _____.

The most important thing I can do today to take me a step closer to my Primary Objective is _____.

My new habit I'm developing (eliminating) is... _____

MORNING THOUGHTS AND INSPIRATIONS

ACTION STEPS FOR TODAY

High Priority

1. _____
2. _____
3. _____

Medium Priority

1. _____
2. _____
3. _____

Low Priority

_____
_____
_____
_____
_____
_____

In which area(s) do I want to improve the most today?

Mental Health

Spiritual Health

Career Health

Physical Health

Social Health

Family Health

Financial Health

Weekly Goal Focus:

Today I am grateful for...

_____
_____
_____
_____
_____
_____
_____
_____
_____

How was my day? Did I feel good about my performance? What did I learn? Did I have a new insight? What would I do differently?

_____
_____
_____
_____
_____
_____
_____
_____

NOTES AND REFLECTIONS FROM TODAY

What was my energy level today? (lowest to highest)   1 2 3 4 5 6 7 8 9 10

If not a "10", what will I do tomorrow to make it closer to a "10"? _____

I ate my frog today: Yes   No

What Time? _____

I did my new habit: Yes   No

What Time? _____

FOR TOMORROW

_____
_____
_____
_____

"We are what we pretend to be, so we must be careful about what we pretend to be."

Kurt Vonnegut

M T W T F S S

Date: _____

MY PRIMARY OBJECTIVE

The most important thing I can do today to take me a step closer to my Primary Objective is _____.

The most important thing I can do today to take me a step closer to my Primary Objective is _____.

The most important thing I can do today to take me a step closer to my Primary Objective is _____.

The most important thing I can do today to take me a step closer to my Primary Objective is _____.

My new habit I'm developing (eliminating) is... _____

MORNING THOUGHTS AND INSPIRATIONS

My biggest frog to eat today...

_____

ACTION STEPS FOR TODAY

High Priority

1. _____
2. _____
3. _____

Medium Priority

1. _____
2. _____
3. _____

Low Priority

_____
_____
_____
_____
_____
_____

In which area(s) do I want to improve the most today?

Mental Health

Spiritual Health

Career Health

Physical Health

Social Health

Family Health

Financial Health

Weekly Goal Focus:

Today I am grateful for...

_____

_____

_____

_____

_____

_____

_____

_____

How was my day? Did I feel good about my performance? What did I learn? Did I have a new insight? What would I do differently?

_____

_____

_____

_____

_____

_____

_____

_____

NOTES AND REFLECTIONS FROM TODAY

What was my energy level today? (lowest to highest) 1 2 3 4 5 6 7 8 9 10

If not a "10", what will I do tomorrow to make it closer to a "10"? _____

I ate my frog today: Yes   No

What Time? _____

I did my new habit: Yes   No

What Time? _____

"Do what you feel in your heart to be right – for you'll be criticized anyway."

Eleanor Roosevelt

FOR TOMORROW

_____

_____

_____

_____

M T W T F S S

Date: _____

MY PRIMARY OBJECTIVE

The most important thing I can do today to take me a step closer to my Primary Objective is _____.

The most important thing I can do today to take me a step closer to my Primary Objective is _____.

The most important thing I can do today to take me a step closer to my Primary Objective is _____.

The most important thing I can do today to take me a step closer to my Primary Objective is _____.

My new habit I'm developing (eliminating) is... _____

MORNING THOUGHTS AND INSPIRATIONS

My biggest frog to eat today...

_____

ACTION STEPS FOR TODAY

High Priority

1. _____
2. _____
3. _____

Medium Priority

1. _____
2. _____
3. _____

Low Priority

_____
_____
_____
_____
_____
_____

In which area(s) do I want to improve the most today?

Mental Health

Spiritual Health

Career Health

Physical Health

Social Health

Family Health

Financial Health

Weekly Goal Focus:

Today I am grateful for...

_____

_____

_____

_____

_____

_____

_____

_____

How was my day? Did I feel good about my performance? What did I learn? Did I have a new insight? What would I do differently?

_____

_____

_____

_____

_____

_____

_____

_____

NOTES AND REFLECTIONS FROM TODAY

What was my energy level today? (lowest to highest) 1 2 3 4 5 6 7 8 9 10

If not a "10", what will I do tomorrow to make it closer to a "10"? _____

I ate my frog today: Yes   No

What Time? _____

I did my new habit: Yes   No

What Time? _____

FOR TOMORROW

_____

_____

_____

_____

"Talent hits a target no one else can hit.
Genius hits a target no one else can see."
Arthur Schopenhauer

DAILY PREVIEW
DAY 82

M T W T F S S

Date: _____

MY PRIMARY OBJECTIVE

[ ]

The most important thing I can do today to take me a step closer to my Primary Objective is _____.

The most important thing I can do today to take me a step closer to my Primary Objective is _____.

The most important thing I can do today to take me a step closer to my Primary Objective is _____.

The most important thing I can do today to take me a step closer to my Primary Objective is _____.

My new habit I'm developing (eliminating) is... _____

MORNING THOUGHTS AND INSPIRATIONS

My biggest frog to eat today...

_____

ACTION STEPS FOR TODAY

High Priority

1. _____
2. _____
3. _____

Medium Priority

1. _____
2. _____
3. _____

Low Priority

_____

_____

_____

_____

_____

_____

In which area(s) do I want to improve the most today?

Mental Health

Spiritual Health

Career Health

Physical Health

Social Health

Family Health

Financial Health

Weekly Goal Focus:

Today I am grateful for...

_____
_____
_____
_____
_____
_____
_____
_____
_____

How was my day? Did I feel good about my performance? What did I learn? Did I have a new insight? What would I do differently?

_____
_____
_____
_____
_____
_____
_____
_____

NOTES AND REFLECTIONS FROM TODAY

What was my energy level today? (lowest to highest) 1 2 3 4 5 6 7 8 9 10

If not a "10", what will I do tomorrow to make it closer to a "10"? _____

I ate my frog today: Yes   No

What Time? _____

I did my new habit: Yes   No

What Time? _____

"I'm the one that's got to die when it's time for me to die, so let me live my life the way I want to."

Jimi Hendrix

FOR TOMORROW

_____
_____
_____
_____

DAILY PREVIEW
DAY 83

M T W T F S S

Date: _____

MY PRIMARY OBJECTIVE

The most important thing I can do today to take me a step closer to my Primary Objective is _____.

The most important thing I can do today to take me a step closer to my Primary Objective is _____.

The most important thing I can do today to take me a step closer to my Primary Objective is _____.

The most important thing I can do today to take me a step closer to my Primary Objective is _____.

My new habit I'm developing (eliminating) is... _____

MORNING THOUGHTS AND INSPIRATIONS

My biggest frog to eat today...

_____

ACTION STEPS FOR TODAY

High Priority

1. _____
2. _____
3. _____

Medium Priority

1. _____
2. _____
3. _____

Low Priority

_____
_____
_____
_____
_____
_____

In which area(s) do I want to improve the most today?

Mental Health

Spiritual Health

Career Health

Physical Health

Social Health

Family Health

Financial Health

Today I am grateful for...

_____
_____
_____
_____
_____
_____
_____
_____
_____

How was my day? Did I feel good about my performance? What did I learn? Did I have a new insight? What would I do differently?

_____
_____
_____
_____
_____
_____
_____
_____
_____

NOTES AND REFLECTIONS FROM TODAY

What was my energy level today? (lowest to highest) 1 2 3 4 5 6 7 8 9 10

If not a "10", what will I do tomorrow to make it closer to a "10"? _____

I ate my frog today: Yes   No

What Time? _____

I did my new habit: Yes   No

What Time? _____

"Always do what you are afraid to do."
Ralph Waldo Emerson

FOR TOMORROW

_____
_____
_____
_____

DAILY PREVIEW
DAY 84

M T W T F S S

Date: _____

MY PRIMARY OBJECTIVE

The most important thing I can do today to take me a step closer to my Primary Objective is _____.

The most important thing I can do today to take me a step closer to my Primary Objective is _____.

The most important thing I can do today to take me a step closer to my Primary Objective is _____.

The most important thing I can do today to take me a step closer to my Primary Objective is _____.

My new habit I'm developing (eliminating) is... _____

MORNING THOUGHTS AND INSPIRATIONS

My biggest frog to eat today...

_____

ACTION STEPS FOR TODAY

High Priority

1. _____
2. _____
3. _____

Medium Priority

1. _____
2. _____
3. _____

Low Priority

_____
_____
_____
_____
_____
_____

In which area(s) do I want to improve the most today?

Mental Health

Spiritual Health

Career Health

Physical Health

Social Health

Family Health

Financial Health

Weekly Goal Focus:

Today I am grateful for...

_____
_____
_____
_____
_____
_____
_____
_____
_____

How was my day? Did I feel good about my performance? What did I learn? Did I have a new insight? What would I do differently?

_____
_____
_____
_____
_____
_____
_____
_____

NOTES AND REFLECTIONS FROM TODAY

What was my energy level today? (lowest to highest) 1 2 3 4 5 6 7 8 9 10

If not a "10", what will I do tomorrow to make it closer to a "10"? _____

I ate my frog today: Yes No

What Time? _____

I did my new habit: Yes No

What Time? _____

FOR TOMORROW

_____
_____
_____
_____

"Imperfection is beauty, madness is genius and it's better to be absolutely ridiculous than absolutely boring."

Marilyn Monroe

WEEKLY CHECK-INS
WEEK 12

The Purpose of the Weekly Check-In is to...

1) Check-in with your progress throughout the week.

2) Re-focus for the upcoming week.

3) Get inspired for the future.

THE CHECK-IN

What have I accomplished since last week? What were the two most important things that I learned this week? Is there anything that I would have done differently? If so, what?

_____

_____

_____

_____

_____

What are my wins or victories since last week?

_____

_____

_____

What's the highlight (or low-light) of my week?

_____

_____

_____

What am I thankful for this week?

_____

_____

_____

The place I feel stuck is

_____

_____

_____

In which area(s) did I grow the most last week?

Mental Health

Spiritual Health

Career Health

Physical Health

Social Health

Family Health

Financial Health

What was my average energy level for the week?

1 2 3 4 5 6 7 8 9 10

What number do I want it to be next week?

1 2 3 4 5 6 7 8 9 10

How often did you eat your frog?

1 2 3 4 5 6 7

On a 1 - 10 scale, 1 being low and 10 being high, how grateful have I been feeling this last week?

1 2 3 4 5 6 7 8 9 10

How did I do with my new habit building/eliminating?

_____

_____

_____

194

Every week, we will be re-focusing on our future life. So, take a moment and fill this in again. There will be a few questions after you finish.

If there were no rules, and I could not fail, what would my life be like?

Describe your future life in detail and in writing...

_____

_____

_____

_____

_____

_____

When you wrote this out again, how did you feel? Were you excited? Were you bored? Did your vision evolve? Was it different than before? Was there more detail or less? Did you even do this exercise? If not, how come?

_____

_____

_____

Look through your future life. Now, fill in the blank...

If I only accomplish _____ next week, my future life would surely come to be.

This is your Primary Objective for the next week.

Take a moment and fill in the days of the week for the next week.

We are coming to the end of this workbook. If you are finding this process valuable, go to Amazon.com or Lulu.com, and order your next Life Alchemy 2.0. This will take you through your next 91 days, and if you do it now, you won't lose any of your momentum.

Go on to Day 85 and be amazing!

DAILY PREVIEW
DAY 85

M T W T F S S

Date: _____

MY PRIMARY OBJECTIVE

☝

The most important thing I can do today to take me a step closer to my Primary Objective is _____.

The most important thing I can do today to take me a step closer to my Primary Objective is _____.

The most important thing I can do today to take me a step closer to my Primary Objective is _____.

The most important thing I can do today to take me a step closer to my Primary Objective is _____.

My new habit I'm developing (eliminating) is... _____

MORNING THOUGHTS AND INSPIRATIONS

My biggest frog to eat today...
_____

ACTION STEPS FOR TODAY ⚐

High Priority
1. _____
2. _____
3. _____

Medium Priority
1. _____
2. _____
3. _____

Low Priority
_____
_____
_____
_____
_____
_____

In which area(s) do I want to improve the most today?

Mental Health

Spiritual Health

Career Health

Physical Health

Social Health

Family Health

Financial Health

Weekly Goal Focus:

Today I am grateful for...

_____
_____
_____
_____
_____
_____
_____
_____

How was my day? Did I feel good about my performance? What did I learn? Did I have a new insight? What would I do differently?

_____
_____
_____
_____
_____
_____
_____
_____

NOTES AND REFLECTIONS FROM TODAY

What was my energy level today? (lowest to highest) 1 2 3 4 5 6 7 8 9 10

If not a "10", what will I do tomorrow to make it closer to a "10"? _____

I ate my frog today: Yes   No

I did my new habit: Yes   No

What Time? _____

What Time? _____

FOR TOMORROW

_____
_____
_____
_____

"First they ignore you, then they ridicule you, then they fight you, and then you win."

Mahatma Gandhi

M T W T F S S

Date: _____

MY PRIMARY OBJECTIVE ☞

[ ]

The most important thing I can do today to take me a step closer to my Primary Objective is _____.

The most important thing I can do today to take me a step closer to my Primary Objective is _____.

The most important thing I can do today to take me a step closer to my Primary Objective is _____.

The most important thing I can do today to take me a step closer to my Primary Objective is _____.

My new habit I'm developing (eliminating) is... _____

MORNING THOUGHTS AND INSPIRATIONS ☀

My biggest frog to eat today...

_____

ACTION STEPS FOR TODAY ⚑

High Priority

1. _____

2. _____

3. _____

Medium Priority

1. _____

2. _____

3. _____

Low Priority

_____

_____

_____

_____

_____

_____

In which area(s) do I want to improve the most today?

Mental Health

Spiritual Health

Career Health

Physical Health

Social Health

Family Health

Financial Health

Weekly Goal Focus:

Today I am grateful for...

_____
_____
_____
_____
_____
_____
_____
_____

How was my day? Did I feel good about my performance? What did I learn? Did I have a new insight? What would I do differently?

_____
_____
_____
_____
_____
_____
_____

NOTES AND REFLECTIONS FROM TODAY

What was my energy level today? (lowest to highest) 1 2 3 4 5 6 7 8 9 10

If not a "10", what will I do tomorrow to make it closer to a "10"? _____

I ate my frog today: Yes   No

What Time? _____

I did my new habit: Yes   No

What Time? _____

FOR TOMORROW

_____
_____
_____
_____

"If you live each day as it was your last, someday you'll most certainly be right"
Steve Jobs

DAILY PREVIEW
DAY 87

M T W T F S S

Date: _____

MY PRIMARY OBJECTIVE ☝

[   ]

The most important thing I can do today to take me a step closer to my Primary Objective is _____.

The most important thing I can do today to take me a step closer to my Primary Objective is _____.

The most important thing I can do today to take me a step closer to my Primary Objective is _____.

The most important thing I can do today to take me a step closer to my Primary Objective is _____.

My new habit I'm developing (eliminating) is... _____

MORNING THOUGHTS AND INSPIRATIONS ☀

[   ]

My biggest frog to eat today...

_____

ACTION STEPS FOR TODAY ⚐

High Priority
1. _____
2. _____
3. _____

Medium Priority
1. _____
2. _____
3. _____

Low Priority
_____
_____
_____
_____
_____
_____

In which area(s) do I want to improve the most today?

Mental Health

Spiritual Health

Career Health

Physical Health

Social Health

Family Health

Financial Health

Weekly Goal Focus:

Today I am grateful for...

_____
_____
_____
_____
_____
_____
_____
_____

How was my day? Did I feel good about my performance? What did I learn? Did I have a new insight? What would I do differently?

_____
_____
_____
_____
_____
_____
_____

NOTES AND REFLECTIONS FROM TODAY

What was my energy level today? (lowest to highest) 1 2 3 4 5 6 7 8 9 10

If not a "10", what will I do tomorrow to make it closer to a "10"? _____

I ate my frog today: Yes   No

What Time? _____

I did my new habit: Yes   No

What Time? _____

FOR TOMORROW

_____
_____
_____
_____

Do what you can, with what you have, where you are."

Theodore Roosevelt

DAILY PREVIEW
DAY 88

M T W T F S S

Date: _____

MY PRIMARY OBJECTIVE

[_____]

The most important thing I can do today to take me a step closer to my Primary Objective is _____.

The most important thing I can do today to take me a step closer to my Primary Objective is _____.

The most important thing I can do today to take me a step closer to my Primary Objective is _____.

The most important thing I can do today to take me a step closer to my Primary Objective is _____.

My new habit I'm developing (eliminating) is... _____

MORNING THOUGHTS AND INSPIRATIONS

My biggest frog to eat today...

_____

ACTION STEPS FOR TODAY

High Priority
1. _____
2. _____
3. _____

Medium Priority
1. _____
2. _____
3. _____

Low Priority
_____
_____
_____
_____
_____
_____

In which area(s) do I want to improve the most today?

Mental Health

Spiritual Health

Career Health

Physical Health

Social Health

Family Health

Financial Health

DAILY REVIEW
DAY 88

Today I am grateful for...

_____
_____
_____
_____
_____
_____
_____
_____
_____
_____

How was my day? Did I feel good about my performance? What did I learn? Did I have a new insight? What would I do differently?

_____
_____
_____
_____
_____
_____
_____
_____
_____

NOTES AND REFLECTIONS FROM TODAY

What was my energy level today? (lowest to highest) 1 2 3 4 5 6 7 8 9 10

If not a "10", what will I do tomorrow to make it closer to a "10"? _____

I ate my frog today: Yes   No

What Time? _____

I did my new habit: Yes   No

What Time? _____

FOR TOMORROW

_____
_____
_____
_____

"I am enough of an artist to draw freely upon my imagination. Imagination is more important than knowledge. Knowledge is limited. Imagination encircles the world."

Albert Einstein

DAILY PREVIEW
DAY 89

M T W T F S S

Date: _____

MY PRIMARY OBJECTIVE

The most important thing I can do today to take me a step closer to my Primary Objective is _____.

The most important thing I can do today to take me a step closer to my Primary Objective is _____.

The most important thing I can do today to take me a step closer to my Primary Objective is _____.

The most important thing I can do today to take me a step closer to my Primary Objective is _____.

My new habit I'm developing (eliminating) is... _____

MORNING THOUGHTS AND INSPIRATIONS

My biggest frog to eat today...

_____

ACTION STEPS FOR TODAY

High Priority

1. _____
2. _____
3. _____

Medium Priority

1. _____
2. _____
3. _____

Low Priority

_____
_____
_____
_____
_____
_____

In which area(s) do I want to improve the most today?

Mental Health

Spiritual Health

Career Health

Physical Health

Social Health

Family Health

Financial Health

Weekly Goal Focus:

Today I am grateful for...

_____
_____
_____
_____
_____
_____
_____
_____

How was my day? Did I feel good about my performance? What did I learn? Did I have a new insight? What would I do differently?

_____
_____
_____
_____
_____
_____
_____
_____

NOTES AND REFLECTIONS FROM TODAY

What was my energy level today? (lowest to highest) 1 2 3 4 5 6 7 8 9 10

If not a "10", what will I do tomorrow to make it closer to a "10"? _____

I ate my frog today: Yes   No

What Time? _____

I did my new habit: Yes   No

What Time? _____

"When things go wrong, don't go with them."

Elvis Presley

FOR TOMORROW

_____
_____
_____
_____

M T W T F S S

Date: _____

MY PRIMARY OBJECTIVE 👉 [_____]

The most important thing I can do today to take me a step closer to my Primary Objective is _____.

The most important thing I can do today to take me a step closer to my Primary Objective is _____.

The most important thing I can do today to take me a step closer to my Primary Objective is _____.

The most important thing I can do today to take me a step closer to my Primary Objective is _____.

My new habit I'm developing (eliminating) is... _____

MORNING THOUGHTS AND INSPIRATIONS ☀

My biggest frog to eat today...

_____

ACTION STEPS FOR TODAY 🚩

High Priority
1. _____
2. _____
3. _____

Medium Priority
1. _____
2. _____
3. _____

Low Priority
_____
_____
_____
_____
_____
_____
_____

In which area(s) do I want to improve the most today?

Mental Health

Spiritual Health

Career Health

Physical Health

Social Health

Family Health

Financial Health

Weekly Goal Focus:

Today I am grateful for...

_____

_____

_____

_____

_____

_____

_____

_____

_____

How was my day? Did I feel good about my performance? What did I learn? Did I have a new insight? What would I do differently?

_____

_____

_____

_____

_____

_____

_____

_____

NOTES AND REFLECTIONS FROM TODAY

What was my energy level today? (lowest to highest) 1 2 3 4 5 6 7 8 9 10

If not a "10", what will I do tomorrow to make it closer to a "10"? _____

I ate my frog today: Yes   No

What Time? _____

I did my new habit: Yes   No

What Time? _____

"You only live once, but if you do it right, once is enough."

Mae West

FOR TOMORROW

_____

_____

_____

_____

M T W T F S S

Date: _____

My biggest frog to eat today...

_____

ACTION STEPS FOR TODAY

MY PRIMARY OBJECTIVE

The most important thing I can do today to take me a step closer to my Primary Objective is _____.

The most important thing I can do today to take me a step closer to my Primary Objective is _____.

The most important thing I can do today to take me a step closer to my Primary Objective is _____.

The most important thing I can do today to take me a step closer to my Primary Objective is _____.

My new habit I'm developing (eliminating) is... _____

MORNING THOUGHTS AND INSPIRATIONS

High Priority

1. _____
2. _____
3. _____

Medium Priority

1. _____
2. _____
3. _____

Low Priority

_____
_____
_____
_____
_____
_____
_____

In which area(s) do I want to improve the most today?

Mental Health

Spiritual Health

Career Health

Physical Health

Social Health

Family Health

Financial Health

Today I am grateful for...

_____
_____
_____
_____
_____
_____
_____
_____
_____

How was my day? Did I feel good about my performance? What did I learn? Did I have a new insight? What would I do differently?

_____
_____
_____
_____
_____
_____
_____
_____

NOTES AND REFLECTIONS FROM TODAY

What was my energy level today? (lowest to highest) 1 2 3 4 5 6 7 8 9 10

If not a "10", what will I do tomorrow to make it closer to a "10"? _____

I ate my frog today: Yes   No

What Time? _____

I did my new habit: Yes   No

What Time? _____

FOR TOMORROW

_____
_____
_____
_____

"Don't cry because it's over, smile because it happened."

Dr. Seuss

WEEKLY CHECK-INS
WEEK 13

The Purpose of the Weekly Check-In is to...

1) Check-in with your progress throughout the week.

2) Re-focus for the upcoming week.

3) Get inspired for the future.

THE CHECK-IN

What have I accomplished since last week? What were the two most important things that I learned this week? Is there anything that I would have done differently? If so, what?

_____
_____
_____
_____
_____

What are my wins or victories since last week?

_____
_____
_____

What's the highlight (or low-light) of my week?

_____
_____
_____

What am I thankful for this week?

_____
_____
_____

The place I feel stuck is

_____
_____
_____

In which area(s) did I grow the most last week?

Mental Health

Spiritual Health

Career Health

Physical Health

Social Health

Family Health

Financial Health

What was my average energy level for the week?

1 2 3 4 5 6 7 8 9 10

What number do I want it to be next week?

1 2 3 4 5 6 7 8 9 10

How often did you eat your frog?

1 2 3 4 5 6 7

On a 1 - 10 scale, 1 being low and 10 being high, how grateful have I been feeling this last week?

1 2 3 4 5 6 7 8 9 10

How did I do with my new habit building/eliminating?

_____
_____
_____

Every week, we will be re-focusing on our future life. So, take a moment and fill this in again. There will be a few questions after you finish.

RE-FOCUS
WEEK 13

If there were no rules, and I could not fail, what would my life be like?

Describe your future life in detail and in writing...

_____
_____
_____
_____
_____
_____
_____

When you wrote this out again, how did you feel? Were you excited? Were you bored? Did your vision evolve? Was it different than before? Was there more detail or less? Did you even do this exercise? If not, how come?

_____
_____
_____

Look through your future life. Now, fill in the blank...

If I only accomplish _____ next week, my future life would surely come to be.

This is your Primary Objective for the next week.

Now What?

CONGRATULATE YOURSELF!

You put in the time. You defined your dream life. You focused on it. You took action towards it. Either you are living your dream life right now, or you are a lot closer to achieving it than you were just 3 months ago.

Way to go!

If you are enjoying Life Alchemy and you are experiencing great changes in your life, keep going. Build this into one of your success habits. Buy another Life Alchemy 2.0 and see how far it will take you.

Also, tell others about the Life Alchemy Process. Can you imagine a whole world of people taking action towards their dreams? How cool would that be? Buy Life Alchemy 1.0 for a loved one today. By the way, if someone bought it for you, make sure to thank them and let them know how you have been able to improve your life with a little Life Alchemy.

Once again, *WAY TO GO!*

ABOUT THE AUTHOR

Dr. Dale Ellwein is an author, lecturer and wellness lifestyle specialist. He received his doctorate in Chiropractic from Life Chiropractic College West in Hayward, California, in 1991, and did advance studies with Dr. James L. Chestnut, earning his Chiropractic Wellness Professional Certification. His book, *Dear Oprah: The Health Book for Everyone*, is a staple for those who care about their health.

Dr. Ellwein inspires people of all ages to achieve peak performance, focus, mental acuity, and amazing health. He teaches simple, proven systems that inspire his patients to eat, move and think in ways that support their longevity and vital, healing nature.

Using the essential combination of lifestyle management and advanced chiropractic care, Dr. Ellwein has helped thousands of individuals overcome aches, pains, and diseases, and improve their overall quality of life. His proven program has been shown to restore health and healing in the bodies of his patients—often leading to long, inspired, joy-filled lives.

Dr. Ellwein practices in Southern California, where he lives with his wife, Barbara, two children, three dogs and six chickens. He conducts extensive talks on optimum performance, health and longevity, and several of his talks, videos, and articles can be found on the internet.

For more information on Dr. Dale Ellwein, go to www.thedoctorofthefuture.com.

www.ingramcontent.com/pod-product-compliance
Lightning Source LLC
Chambersburg PA
CBHW080501110426
42742CB00017B/2967